JEZA'S JESUS JUICE

JEZA'S JESUS JUICE

A Drag Queen's Christian Devotional

by JEZA BELLE

RESOURCE *Publications* · Eugene, Oregon

JEZA'S JESUS JUICE
A Drag Queen's Christian Devotional

Resource Publications
An Imprint of Wipf and Stock Publishers
199 W. 8th Ave., Suite 3
Eugene, OR 97401

www.wipfandstock.com

PAPERBACK ISBN: 979-8-3852-0709-1
HARDCOVER ISBN: 979-8-3852-0710-7
EBOOK ISBN: 979-8-3852-0711-4

Dedication

To the LGBTQ+ souls who have walked this earth before me and endured so that I could freely be who I am today.

To the love of my life, and my God-given gift of a partner. No one could be more blessed than me in this department.

To my mother who gave me religion and raised me to be a proud Jewish-Christian.

Acknowledgements

God- who knows all and is through all.
My poor husband- for reading this 8,000 times.
Dylan Garity- fabulous editor.
Thomas Evans Photography- for always making this mess look so good.
Wipf and Stock- Thank you for taking this journey with me.

Table of Contents

Preface

WARNING: UNLIKE MOST SPIRITUAL or devotional books, this one is peppered with some salty language in places, as well as some spicy content. Hey, I've got a messy reputation to uphold! I've given you notice, so let us proceed.

Looking back throughout my life, I cannot remember a single moment when I didn't not only *believe* in God's existence but *knew* his existence to be so. God calls himself "I AM" in Genesis, and that was ever true in my knowledge of him from my own human genesis. He was there because HE IS. Belief or lack thereof altered nothing about his being.

The same can be said for the relationship I have with "I AM." It exists. The thoughts of other people, whether they think God is real, whether they think someone gay can follow him, or anything else, are irrelevant and play no role in its reality. My life was connected at birth to a powerful Trinity: God the father, Jesus the son and savior, and the Holy Spirit that plays a pivotal role in guiding and speaking to the other parts of this trinity in ways that only spirit can. Mankind, other than the one man who was also God, holds no power over this connection.

I begin with these two thoughts on God's existence and my relationship with him for several reasons that lay out what this book is and is not meant to be.

Jeza's Jesus Juice is a devotional book for those who believe in God. It's a welcome space for those seeking to strengthen the most important relationship one could ever have. It's also a haven for those who have a budding or curious interest but need a point of entry and don't always feel safe exploring such a relationship in traditional settings out of fear.

This book is not, however, a place for debate about whether or not God is real, nor is it ground zero for arguments over whether or not one can be both gay and Christian. There are numerous venues and spaces outside of these pages for those discussions.

To be frank, for too long, hot-mess human beings have stood as gate-keepers, believing they have some kind of power to determine who is worthy of knowing Christ and developing a relationship with God. As a result, across two millennia, untold millions of people have been turned away, chastised and bullied from pulpits, and made to believe that they were "less than." People who didn't meet certain criteria were told they would always be on the outside when it came to being embraced by God. My heart bleeds for these people, because nothing could be further from the truth.

In this book, we leave all of that historical BS and the thoughts of mere mortals at the door and start simply with the truth that always was and always will be: God is, and you can have a wonderful and deep relationship with him if you choose to do so.

It would be silly if I didn't take a moment to confront head-on the question that is bound to be at the forefront of any reader's mind here—why in the world is a drag queen writing a Christian devotional book and using her stage name, which happens to also be the name of one of the most wicked women in the Bible?

To address the first part of the question, I'd like to point out that the American-Political- "Christian"-Movement has made drag queens the lepers of the day. With that in mind, there is frankly no better way to point out the hollow religious hypocrisy of our very own Pharisees than by lifting up the power of God through Christ via those they consider to be the most unclean.

To the later part of the question, when I started drag, I took on the name of Jeza Belle for the very reason I write this book today. I wanted to highlight that it's often those we consider to be the weakest, the worst, the most vile, whom God moves through, and through whom he demonstrates his immense power. One need only look at the apostle Paul, who was a murderer of Christians, to see how God takes those on the farthest fringes and works through them in ways we are too short-sighted to comprehend. Why not work through a man wearing women's clothing, donning the name of the worst woman in scripture? Not that I'm anything that should be remotely worthy of being a vessel. Then again, none of his vessels ever were, and that's because it's about him, not the packaging through which he demonstrates his power.

Granted, as a performer, I lean toward bawdy and blue comedy. Some might question how a potty- mouthed comedian could be sharing such a pure message. Truth be told, I think God has an absolutely wicked sense of humor. We are made in his image, after all, and quite frankly I don't think God is even remotely as uptight and puckered up as most of us think. He has the ability and comedic genius to move through a drag queen, just as he moved through Deborah in the Bible at great shame to the male judges of the time, while likely having a great big giant belly laugh at those limited enough to not see the message that was being sent.

Jeza's Jesus Juice is laid out as follows. Each chapter begins with some scripture, almost always from the New International Version (NIV), unless otherwise noted. One can't ground themselves or grow their relationship with God without hearing from him directly. Do note, I encourage everyone to read the Bible outside of these pages. It's so incredibly important to under-stand context, who was being spoken to at the time and why, and to make yourself intimately acquainted with the arc of the biblical story of God, his working through the Jewish people, the powerful full-circle journey of the Messiah and Savior Jesus, and the spreading of his message that brings us through to where we are today. All of that is to say that we will isolate and expound on Bible verses, but you should really go beyond two or three sentences to understand anything in depth. Study and read for yourself, be-cause none of us imperfect people should be the ultimate stopgap for God himself. He alone will judge and no one else, so get to know him outside of just listening to the voices of others.

After the scripture, I will basically rant, which will include different things such as the provision of some historical perspective, background to the text, personal stories, and connections to the power of the Word. In some chapters, I will keep it lighter, while others may be heavier with what's known as apologetics, or a defense of the Christian faith, but from a view-point of inclusivity. Traditional apologetics defends God's existence. My defense will be of God's inclusive love, though again not with the purpose of arguing any point to a fault—in my eyes, that distracts from developing your relationship with God and instead leaves your energy on arguing with people who seek to block that relationship.

These thoughts will be followed up with prayers. Feel free to read or recite them as they are or to use them as springboards in developing your own communication with God.

Last, I will pose several questions to allow readers to delve deeper into their own thoughts on the topics addressed in the pages that follow. These will hopefully allow room for personal spiritual growth.

You now have the purpose and the plan, so let's get juiced!

God's Word

"For the word of God is alive and active. Sharper than any double-edged sword, it penetrates even to dividing soul and spirit, joints and marrow; it judges the thoughts and attitudes of the heart."

—Hebrews 4:12

I planned to end this book with a chapter on God's word; however, the closer I found myself to the conclusion of my writing, the more obvious it became that I needed to start with this chapter, not close with it. Everything that follows in these pages is predicated on a strong belief in the power of scripture. Within the covers of what is widely accepted as today's biblical canon are words of life and strength that demonstrate clearly the arc of our history as beings and God's role as creator and ever-loving Father.

One might imagine that a drag artist, a member of the LGBTQ+ community, would be running from, not to, scripture to find solace, comfort, and purpose. Yet, the word of God transcends sexuality, gender, race, creed, and any number of other things that separate us on this earthly plane.

Instead, it is through his word that I find the humility to fall on my face before his greatness. I also find the purpose to stand up and be counted as a follower of Christ, and ultimately, I find myself filled with love overflowing that compels me to share it with others, especially the weak and outcast.

The verse from Hebrews that leads off this chapter is enough to send shivers down one's spine— the words God speaks do something nothing else in the universe is able to. These words go right into the very fabric of our being. They cut down past all of the flesh that makes up our bodies, finding their way into our minds, hearts, and souls.

We feel many things deeply in our beings—even things like music and poetry can stir something unseen. Yet, God's word goes further. It is so incredible that it has the ability to separate our souls and spirits. According to the scripture above, it slices so thinly and so deeply that it can differentiate between your inner emotional self and your inner spiritual self.

There exists no other object, tangible or abstract, with the potency, force, or ability to pierce through to our innermost essence in the way that the words of the one who created that essence can.

In the book of Isaiah, God states that his word cannot come back void. This means anything he speaks (and anything you read in scripture is his speaking) is unable to be stopped from accomplishing his will, or his purpose.

Damn, that is eye-popping and terrifying, because it is powerfully infinite. Unstoppable. Final. It is for those reasons I have no choice but to begin here.

For gays, lesbians, transgender people, and the rest of our rainbow community, people have often used the words of scripture to self-inflate, or to tear down and harm us. My main point in writing this devotional book is to counter that ungodly behavior, so that you the reader can spend time reflecting on the words yourself.

Marginalized people have sat by for centuries, and often cowered in fear, while others use God's word as an excuse and a means to hurt anyone they believe is unclean. Sadly, in doing so, those others don't just pour burning coals on their own heads—they push so many wonderful people away from looking into the word of God for themselves.

Here in these pages, I reclaim Christ for all through the words of the Father.

Jesus said, "Man shall not live on bread alone, but on every word that comes from the mouth of God."

So here we begin, because in order to live life to the fullest, in order to have the deep and loving relationship with God that is waiting for us, we first have to be alive, and that life starts by hearing his word. Hearing it directly from him. Pondering it. Dwelling on it. Letting it seep through to our core and find us in those quiet spaces.

Life does not come from Abigail Asswipe from Albuquerque's interpretation. It does not begin or end because Pastor Pete from Plymouth says it is such. It comes from God himself. Wherever you are in the journey of your relationship with God, whether it's been minutes, days, months, years, or decades, going back to his words over and over again and dwelling on them, not man's interpretation of them, is where that intimate relationship starts and ends.

When I first came out, a member of the church I attended reached out to me and said that now that I had fallen into sin and was lost to God, she was praying for me. My response to her was that I was praying for her as well, because God and I were just fine. In fact, our relationship was closer than ever. I was praying that in her journey, she grew to the point where she no longer put God into a box, because he was too big for such small thoughts. For each line of scripture that she threw at me, I threw back two more. She hung up on me!

When gay marriage was being debated in the early 2000s, somehow I ended up in an argument with someone at the James Dobson Focus on the Family Foundation, the conservative evangelical group that was advocating in political circles for legislation that backed their eternal "obsessed with homosexual anal sex" point of view. Incidentally, this topic really seems to preoccupy these supposedly "straight" and very homophobic men of God. However, that is a subject for public bathrooms, massage parlors, sex escort workers' journals, and a different book.

One of their people, I have no clue who, was angrily listing scripture to me on the sin that is homosexuality. He was not prepared for my response explaining the power of God through this word, the love of Jesus, and the lack of any statement from Christ himself on gay men. This particular mouthpiece for the foundation practically lost his mind, and he left the conversation completely dumbfounded

I have no interest whatsoever in playing a tit-for-tat exchange of Bible verses with anyone. Nor is my plan to arm you with biblical passages with which you can swat back at those who consider themselves our enemies. What I am interested in is encouraging each of us in the gay community to jump into the word ourselves. Study it. Research the passages that interest us in terms of who was being spoken to at the time, what was culturally relevant to that group, and under what context the words were given.

Take ownership of your own learning and growth, and under no circumstances allow anyone to tell you that you are somehow too "icky" to have God's presence in and through your life. Take back the power that God gave to each of us to know him for ourselves through his words to us, not through the words of other people. If it was up to them, we would likely all be rounded up and tossed into the fire. Thankfully, it is not.

Jesus himself said, "Heaven and earth will pass away, but my words will never pass away." With so much weight that they are able to punch through the continuum of space and time, yet with an energy so nimble they can deftly slice between our soul and spirit, we owe it to ourselves to tap into God's words.

PRAYER

Infinite Lord, as I spend time reflecting on your words, may they penetrate to the deepest part of my being. I pray, Holy Father, that these words that slice between my soul and spirit seep down into my bones and marrow and bring me peace, understanding, and a growing love for you.

REFLECTION

1. How much of the Bible have I read through?

2. What realistic commitment can I make to consistently reading the word? Daily, weekly, monthly?

3. What areas in the Bible do I want to learn more about? Are there certain topics, books, or passages that I might want to focus on? Which of these would I place first for study, and why?

Radical Inclusivity

"There is neither Jew nor Gentile, neither slave nor free, nor is there male and female, for you are all one in Christ Jesus."

—GALATIANS 3:28

Confession: I wanted to be a minister, but who would have listened to an effeminate gay man talking about God from the pulpit? So, I became the next best thing . . . a drag queen!

The conservative political movement in the United States has somehow managed to displace the agenda of Christ. Unfortunately, this movement's message is not limited to these American shores, but also resonates and influences others around the globe. LGBTQ+ people are assaulted constantly by a barrage of hatred from seemingly unhinged lunatics. These "Christians" bark incessantly on every form of media, where they claim to speak for God and tell us how he has no room for anyone who looks or acts differently than their textbook model of a Christian. Of course, when you dive beneath the surface, you find instead that they are the ones who are poor representatives for Christ.

Before I go further, for the purpose of this devotional, when I say "evangelical," I rather untraditionally mean those rigid members of churches both Protestant *and* Catholic where the preacher/minister and congregation rail from the pulpit and the pews about homosexuality and gender identity. These include but are not limited to Baptists, churches of Christ, many apostolic congregations, major movements within the American black church, numerous nondenominational congregations, the Church of England (partial equality is not equality), various Catholic hierarchy, split movements within major Protestant denominations, etc. Basically any church where even a soft disdain for the LGBTQ+ community is either actively promoted or even tolerated.

One of the primary reasons for this devotional book is to provide a space for LGBTQ+ people, who do not fit into the narrow boxes that these evangelicals create, to safely commune with God without feeling like we do so only as cheeky crashers of God's party. Instead, we will take a deeper look together at how we are not drifters who came in unexpectedly off the street, but rather we are primary guests with a golden invitation sent to us from God himself through Jesus Christ. We are not intruders—we have each been offered a seat at his table that no mere man can deny us.

While there are numerous biblical verses to choose from when it comes to the welcome and loving open arms that Christ extends to us, I went with the Galatians verse above for its shocking and radical inclusivity that rocked the ancient world and still sends ripples across the waters of time today.

Let us begin with some heavy biblical history. In fact, take a sip of something strong. I've personally got an extra-dirty martini in my left hand as I type with my right, as this will take a few intense, alcohol-guzzling paragraphs. For an extra treat, prepare yourself my signature *Jeza's Jesus Juice* cocktail—I've placed the recipe at the back of this book! (This can also be made as a mocktail for anyone who wants to skip the booze.) Hey, if Jesus can turn water into the wine, why can't I provide you with a good libation to slug back?

The apostle Paul wrote the words in Galatians to address a growing controversy in which Jewish- Christians believed that Gentile-Christians need to be circumcised and follow Jewish law. To give context, Jesus the Messiah came as promised to and through the Jewish people, whom God chose to share his message and glory. The long and short of it is that the Jews were the vehicle for the eventual freeing message for all of mankind. When Christ arrived, he began tearing down the centuries-old divides set up through the Judaic sacrificial religious system that excluded non- Jews, or Gentiles, from being covered or saved by God, unless they converted and followed Jewish law and Jewish traditions.

Once Jesus was crucified, the open invitation he made to all people, including non-Jews, began to spread around the world. This led to a number of Gentiles becoming followers of Christ and his Father, the Jewish god Yahweh. While it seems common today for millions of non-Jews to follow God, who had a special relationship with the Jewish people, and through

God's son who was born, died, and rose from the dead a Jew himself, this was a groundbreaking shift at the time.

As Gentiles joined the Jews in following Christ, Jewish-Christians were admittedly uncomfortable with having Gentiles in the fold, especially if the Gentile-Christians did not follow Jewish laws and customs. It's important to note that all of the Apostles and the earliest followers of Jesus were 100 percent Jewish, just as, again, Jesus himself was born into this world Jewish. Since the first Christians were Jews, they followed both Jewish customs and practices while following Christ as their Messiah, or savior, at the same time.

The conflict over how one could possibly be a Gentile and be allowed to follow Jesus the Jewish Messiah eventually led to a message from God to the apostle Peter via a dream, as relayed in the book of Acts. In the dream, God reveals to Peter, using food as symbolism, that Gentiles are fully welcome into the new covenant.

Now we come to Paul's words in Galatians, which were written only a few years later. These particular words were meant to quash a debate over whether or not Gentiles needed to follow Jewish law. Paul makes the point that whatever anyone was before they accepted Christ is unimportant. There is no separation, there are no more or less worthy followers—everyone is welcome and equal, and following Jesus trumps all other concerns. There exists no one group or one type of person better than or over the other. Subsequently, it is not for one group to tell another group how to follow God their way. It does not matter if you are uncircumcised, a slave, a woman, or frankly do not follow the traditions that men lay out as imperatives to knowing and following God. All are welcome; all are equal.

This was earth-shatteringly new after centuries upon centuries of separation. Endless years of people being separated into categories. Centuries of there being a hierarchical order in both Jewish and non-Jewish societies of who was above, below, acceptable, and unacceptable in comparison to each other by how they were born, what path they followed, and what actions they took. I often ponder the similarity of this verse to the culture wars of today. Insert any and all of the LGBTQ+ population into this scripture, and most of today's nonsensical arguments become pointless. Of course, Paul could have gone on at the time and included in his letter to the Galatians a list of every single group that would be outside the norm just as the Gentiles were, but why bother? The verse encapsulates the whole message of

Christianity, in that Jesus was both for and in all followers, not just the ones mankind decided were worthy.

If you have ever stepped a toe into a gay bar, you know how it can often feel like two worlds. On the one hand, a gay bar projects a feeling of unity and acceptance—it is a safe space for anyone whose sexual and/or gender identity might put them at risk in other places.

On the other hand, a gay bar is also a place where we divide quite easily into cliques. People chat with those they come to the bar with, frequently ignoring the strangers around them unless they deem someone particularly attractive.

Often, a number of people stand around the edges of the room, on the fringes. Being a solo flier in a gay bar can sometimes feel quite lonely. One spends their time on the periphery, hoping for someone to welcome you into their conversation. You search from face to face, awaiting an invitation. Those who do not fit our idealized version of physical beauty, or people who might be older than the rest of the patrons, etc., are given a loud and clear message: they are not wanted here, or at least they are only wanted at a very far distance.

Time and again, though, you find someone who flits into a bar and, while they may not fit what our culture deems as particularly fit and therefore worthy of a stool, they blow in like a hurricane of personality and take that seat anyway. They do not await the invitation of others to speak—they talk to whomever they want, and this is frequently met with interest and openness from those who might ordinarily not speak to anyone outside their bar circle or clique. They claim their place where it would otherwise not be offered.

It is like this with God's table when it comes to LGBTQ+ Christians. We often stay back from the table. We do not own our faith, based on very real fears that we are not welcome at God's table by its other occupants. However, those at the table neither created the table nor sent out the invitations. They are not in any way the host.

Christ's radical inclusivity extends way beyond what modern evangelicals tout. At God's table, a seat for each of us exists. This includes you, us, anyone, no matter who we love, what gender we identify as, whether we are a Jew or a Gentile—the list goes on and on, because ultimately, absolutely none of this matters. The table is long and wide. It seats many from all walks who have one common thread: a belief in and love for God. If you have faith in God the Father through Jesus the Son, that seat is yours. Don't be afraid to take it!

The other diners and their perspectives on your worthiness are irrelevant. They can stick their noses in the air, gnash their teeth, and foam at the mouth in unfounded righteous indignation until Christ returns. Yet God Himself invited you to sit, and as such, man cannot ever take that invitation away.

You are welcome, and equal to anyone who sits at the Lord's table! He is radically inclusive of all. Embrace that invite. Don your finest, strap on some falsies, tuck it up, or come to the party in leather or rags. Whatever you do, enter, sit, and feast all the same, basking in the incredible love that is God.

PRAYER

Father in heaven, thank you for sending Jesus for all of us. We are all invited to your table, and you embrace us for who we are, whom we love, and whatever gender identity we ascribe to, because none of that is relevant in Christ. Christ himself and the love you have for us through Him is what is most important. There is no Jew or Gentile, no slave or free, only us humbled before your throne. Please help me, God, to take the seat at your table that you have prepared for me. You know and love me for me, and for that I thank and praise you. In the name of Jesus, Amen.

REFLECTION

1. What has held me back from developing a deeper/closer relationship with God?

2. What can I commit to in order to begin to grow this relationship?

3. Are there resources (people, publications, scriptures) I can rely on to help me on this journey? If so, name what they are and the potential impact they possess?

Mercy Given

"For He says to Moses, "I will have mercy on whom I have mercy and I will have compassion on whom I have compassion." It does not therefore depend on human desire or effort, but on God's mercy."

—ROMANS 9:15–16

Some of my favorite lines from the Bible are the ones above, written by Paul in a letter to the Romans, in which he restates what God said to Moses in Exodus 33:19. At the original time of the quote, God was responding to Moses's request for the Lord to continue to show his presence to and among his people on their journey out of Egypt into the promised land, despite his justifiable fury with the Israelites over their worshiping of the golden calf.

God responded to Moses's request positively but put him on notice by saying that while he could at any moment choose to destroy the Israelites in his anger over their recent idol worship, ultimately he would remain among them and "have mercy on whom I have mercy."

When God the creator tells man that he alone is the judge of those who break his laws, and that he may forgive them if he chooses to do so, I strongly believe that we should tremble before those words. I'd poop my pants before I would want to even feign to have the final choice over man's fate in place of God.

Many evangelicals, when reading the book of Romans, land in the first chapter and then pitch their tents there permanently, never getting to the whole story of the letter Paul wrote to the Romans. They subsequently use the chapter as the justifying verses to lead their attacks on gay people.

Let's take a gander at some of this chapter, shall we?

"The wrath of God is being revealed from heaven against all the god-lessness and wickedness of people, who suppress the truth by their wicked-ness, since what may be known about God is plain to them, because God has made it plain to them. For since the creation of the world God's invisible qualities—his eternal power and divine nature—have been clearly seen, being understood from what has been made, so that people are without excuse... Therefore God gave them over in the sinful desires of their hearts to sexual impurity for the degrading of their bodies with one another. They exchanged the truth about God for a lie, and worshiped and served created things rather than the Creator—who is forever praised. Amen.

Because of this, God gave them over to shameful lusts. Even their women exchanged natural sexual relations for unnatural ones. In the same way the men also abandoned natural relations with women and were inflamed with lust for one another. Men committed shameful acts with other men, and re-ceived in themselves the due penalty for their error." (Romans 1:18–27).

To begin with, one cannot help but immediately be taken right back to the Levitical laws and the connected acts of homosexuality that were tied to idol worship. Indeed, Paul seems to be going back to the beginning in this chapter. The entire book of Romans has a habit of circling back like that and reminding us of the entire arc of the Christian faith. That being, Israelites were called to be separated from those around them and to not do what the Gentiles did. Hence, we land right back to the insistence that you do not worship idols.

To me, the first chapter of Romans is not so much about homosexual acts in the general sense, but rather in the specific sense that God sat by and watched the ancients throw themselves onto pagan altars and worship nonexistent gods through acts of sex. Paul attacks those who are blind to still not see the existence of God at this point. It is not necessarily that Paul condemns homosexuality as the ultimate evil that leads people to eternal judgment, but rather he condemns the denial of God's existence.

If we read on, we find that Paul takes it much further in the next few verses, making it clear that he is not writing about homosexuality as some sort of exclusive evil, but rather about man's refusal to see God and become self-obsessed.

"Furthermore, just as they did not think it worthwhile to retain the knowledge of God, so God gave them over to a depraved mind, so that they do what ought not to be done. They have become filled with every kind of wickedness, evil, greed and depravity. They are full of envy, murder, strife,

deceit and malice. They are gossips, slanderers, God-haters, insolent, arrogant and boastful; they invent ways of doing evil; they disobey their parents; they have no understanding, no fidelity, no love, no mercy. Although they know God's righteous decree that those who do such things deserve death, they not only continue to do these very things but also approve of those who practice them." (Romans 1:28–32).

Most LGBTQ+-hating evangelicals wind up completely missing the mark on these verses, purposefully omitting the acts listed that they engage in daily, including arrogance, insolence, and a lack of understanding, love, or mercy. My my my . . . I guess these don't count? Hard to focus on mercy when all you can think about are gay men and women in the throes of sexual passion. I keep getting the feeling that the arguments centered on Romans 1 are about the sexual repression that causes so many of these very same barkers to be sucking people off in the church stall only to return to the pulpit to have fits of rage about homosexuality. Yes, I said it! I've seen enough pants around ankles and heard enough slurps from parish bathrooms to make a soccer mom blush.

Now that we've dealt with the first chapter of Romans, let's look at the book's much deeper meaning. Romans 9:15–16 for example, point to the book's real message about the supremacy of Christ.

In fact, one of the most prominent features of the book of Romans is that it contends once again with the Jewish and Gentile issue that we touched on earlier, but this time it does it on the flip. Instead of being written to Jewish-Christians who had great difficulty dealing with the idea that one could be Gentile, follow Jesus the Messiah, and not follow Jewish laws and customs, Paul is addressing Gentile-Christians who believed falsely that the Jews had completely fallen out of favor with God and were now replaced entirely in his favor by Gentile-Christians.

Paul, though, checks that point by reminding the Gentiles that while the invitation from Christ is open to all, Gentile-Christians should always and respectfully remember that they are but branches that grow out of the tree that is Israel. Branches do not live without roots. So, in that way, they are attached to and depend on the Jewish roots of the tree.

Basically, Paul was saying that Gentiles should not get a big head and dare to think that they were now the judges over any Jews who did not believe in or follow their Messiah, Jesus.

Instead, God would be the final judge as to who is saved and who is not—Jew, Gentile, or otherwise.

Full circle then. Whether looking at the books of the Torah, when God told the Israelites to separate themselves from the other nations by not worshiping gods that do not actually exist, or when he was annoyed with them for doing just that by creating and bowing to a golden calf, or further on when in the book of Romans, Christians argued over who was saved, Paul's message rings clear. We are not God, but his subjects, and we should remember that.

Paul addresses man's error when it comes to God's mercy in Romans 9:15, but he brings it home in verse 16, where he declares that mercy and compassion have nothing to do with what man thinks, desires, or does. It is a sizzling rebuke that screams out to us to remember our station.

Whenever we get the urge to start declaring who will go to heaven and who is condemned to hell, God's words should echo in our ears: "I will have mercy on whom I have mercy."

God himself will ultimately decide who is in his favor and to whom he shows mercy and compassion, not anyone else, regardless of how they interpret any verse in any book.

If God decides he will have mercy on Jews, he will have mercy on Jews. If God decides he will have mercy on Gentiles, he will have mercy on Gentiles. If God decides he welcomes all to the table, he welcomes all to the table. Whatever humans say is irrelevant. We need to stop fawning over ourselves and start getting out of God's way.

We should throw ourselves on the floor and beg for mercy whenever we dare to proclaim who can and who cannot be saved, whenever we declare who God loves and who God does not. In doing so, we not only give ourselves over to real depravity—the replacement of the Lord above—but we also place ourselves in the line of fire for mercy denied, not granted.

When prominent political figures on either side of the left-right aisle pass away, we often get flooded with memes celebrating their trips straight to hell. While I'm always one for a good meme, and I love a good laugh, I also try to keep these verses in Romans 9 in mind.

In the end, God decides. I imagine when we make it to heaven, we will be shocked by those standing around his throne. I readily expect heaven to be filled with a variety of souls that man cast aside, probably people of differing backgrounds and religious beliefs whom we said would be burning in fiery pits. What will we say then? Will we question his mercy or beg forgiveness for our short-sightedness?

I have a friend who lives in Singapore. He's a gay Christian. Quiet and unassuming, he is the embodiment of faith in action. He uses a large portion of the money he makes from his middle- income job to buy food for the poor. I often see him online delivering food and goods to the elderly and families with children who cannot afford to feed their young. He even makes beautiful crosses with his own hands and hands them out with the food and goods. Frankly, he's a Mother Teresa figure, but most people do not know this about him. He goes from door to door telling people that he does these good works in Jesus's name.

Our society of hypocritical, white-washed tombs would readily say that while what he is doing is nice, he is going to hell because he sleeps with men. I wonder, when both the hypocrite and this doer of good deeds in the name of Jesus stand before God's judgment, what will the outcome be?

Will the white-washed tomb who is saved by the blood of Jesus be cast aside by God because he did not show mercy or demonstrate the love of Christ? This person spent his few and limited breaths spreading a hostile message—that God is waiting to cast those who do not procreate with the opposite sex to eternal damnation.

Will the gay man who is also saved by the blood of Jesus and does good deeds spreading his name far and wide be cast aside because he sleeps with other men?

Will both be saved because they are both Christians?

The answer is ultimately way above my pay grade and yours.

This is the perfect time for me to make a major point. People ask me often if I think those who don't believe in Jesus, follow other religions, or are atheist are going to hell on the day of judgment. Um, it is not *my* job or *my* call to decide for anyone who is not a Christian, follows a different religion, or perhaps has no religion at all what their fate is. I can barely decide if I'm wearing a kitten pump or hooker heels tonight. I am in no position to cast ultimate judgment on anyone whatsoever.

I believe the Bible makes clear in numerous places how those outside "the law" are a law unto themselves, meaning that is where their judgment lies. They are ruled and determined by their own acts in relation to God. So who am I in any way to pretend to be God and declare that Buddhists, Muslims, Hindus, or anyone else will go to hell at judgment? I expect to see many of these wonderful people in heaven too! Even if I *were* to declare who was bound to the fires, my words, and anyone else's, would have no weight in the final hour.

Let us stop pretending to be God. Let us also stop standing in the way of other people knowing God. LGBTQ+ friends and family, let us also stop letting others stand in our way of building that relationship with God ourselves. God said you are someone He loves and welcomes. That is more than enough.

May we constantly remember, God gives mercy to whomever he wants. We, and no one else made of flesh and blood, can ever take that mercy, just like the invitation, away.

PRAYER

I fall before the throne of God, knowing that your mercy is given by you alone. Let me hold on to that mercy, Lord, and never be turned away from it, regardless of whatever words or deeds others throw my way. Your mercy is a force that destroys all attempts to deny me the opportunity you have given me to know and be loved by you.

REFLECTION

1. Where in my life have others shown me mercy?

2. Where in the lives of others can I offer more mercy?

3. When I reflect on the scripture shared at the beginning of this chapter, where do I see it fitting into my life and my beliefs?

Protection

"The angel of the Lord encamps around those who fear Him, and He delivers them."

—PSALMS 34:7

Three years ago, my mother had a tumor removed from her brain. During the first year of her long, slow (and still not completed) recovery, she would comment on things that the rest of us could not see. One day, I was on the phone with my her and she said, "You know they are with you everywhere, especially when you ride the subway."

Come again? I asked my mother who she was talking about.

"I know you won't believe me, but they are there with you," my mother explained. "There are four, I guess you can call them men, but they are really angels. They are very tall, like seven feet and strong! One stands before you, one behind you, and one on either side of you. God sent them, and they protect you wherever you go, and I want you to know they ride with you on the subway to make sure no one ever bothers you. You are always safe."

I thanked her for sharing and agreed that while some things are probably beyond our sight, I did know that I was protected by God at all times.

Several months later, I was riding on a subway train, out of drag, at five o'clock in the morning. I was sitting on the very first bench at the start of one of the train's cars. Commute populations can vary, meaning some days the train can be packed at 5 a.m., and on other days I could be the only one in the car. On this particular morning, the train was hopping.

I got on and took my seat and began reading something on my phone. When the subway car stopped at the next station, a crazy man, for lack of a better or more clinically appropriate term, entered all the way at the far end of the car.

The man started to work his way down the subway car as it rolled out of the station. He stopped to scream, curse, and make violent threats directly into the faces of each of the twenty or so individuals sitting along the way, who were trying to mind their business and get to wherever they were headed.

The screamer did not miss a single person on his way down the car, and the passengers looked terrified for their lives.

When this man finally made his way to my end of the train, his body moved slowly in my direction. I could see him out of the corner of my eye. He was within two feet of me when suddenly he stopped in his tracks. Said crazy man then backed up several feet while looking directly at me, before stopping at the nearest set of doors and proceeding to mumble to himself and curse under his breath.

The train slowed to a stop, and the doors opened. The man dashed out of the subway car onto the platform, and we pulled away.

At first, I chuckled to myself that I must have looked even crazier than he did, and he figured he'd better not mess with me! After all, he had hollered and carried on so confrontationally toward each of the other passengers, except for me.

Then, I remembered my mother's words. I wondered if just because I could not see these four angels protecting me, "especially on the subway," it did not mean they were not actually there.

Reflecting back further, I realize there have been so many times in my life where, but for the grace and protection of God, I should have been toast. Were there angels encamped around me then as well? The bank robbery with the gun in my face, the gunshots that flew past me on a hunting trip, the accident where my father's truck rolled over, the time my tire was ripped off of my car on a highway and my car just gently stopped on the side of the road, and on and on and on.

Once, a number of years back, I was in a bar in a country in South America. I was talking to a guy and literally had just taken one tiny drink from the beer I had ordered. The next minute, I remember being led through the streets of the city, with this man "helping" me back to my hotel room. My very next memory was when I woke up the next morning naked.

I had been roofied.

But for the protection of God himself, I do not know to this day how I survived. I was in a foreign country, drugged, and passed out. Absolutely anything could have happened.

Not only was I alive, but my assailant barely took any of my belongings except for a Mickey Mouse T-shirt and a cheap watch. He left my passport and my money, and by the feel of my body and later STD testing, apparently he had not taken advantage of me sexually either. All I did know was that I was alive and relatively unharmed. Embarrassed, yes. Dead, no.

This is not to say that had I been raped, God would not have been with me and protecting me, mind you. Plus, the fact is, caca happens to all of us in this world, so to speak, even to Christians. No one walks out unscathed. Yet God is in control no matter what happens, even if it is the worst thing imaginable. Therefore, I walk in the knowledge that he's protecting me both physically and spiritually at all times. This doesn't mean I run into the fire because I know I am safe, as I am fairly certain he expects me to use the brainpower I was given to try to avoid certain situations, if possible, but not everything can be avoided. Knowing that there's one or possibly a host of angels on every side of me, or even the direct hand of God himself cupping me in protection, gives me great peace at all times and in all things.

You, like me, are not alone. Bad things may still happen, because that's the natural order of the world, but God has your back. You cannot get any safer than in the hands of the one that created you.

PRAYER

Lord, you surround me with your protection in many forms. Though I may not always see you there, I take comfort knowing that my human eyes have limitations, but your power knows no such limits. Let me lean comfortably into the knowledge that you are my greatest defense and defender in all things.

REFLECTION

1. At which times in my life have I felt especially protected?

2. During which times have I felt the most vulnerable?

3. In what ways can I call on God now to provide protection to me?

Forgiveness Given to Us

"Blessed is he whose transgressions are forgiven, whose sins are covered."
—PSALMS 32:1

Forgiveness is like a three-sided figure. There's forgiveness given to us, forgiveness we give to others, and forgiveness we need to extend to ourselves. The latter sides are grounded in the first, the base of it all, and so we begin there.

A central theme of Judeo-Christianity is the disastrous, yet special, nature of mankind. We are complete wrecks on the one hand, barreling through the universe at a thousand miles an hour. Busy little beings on a spinning orb whose lives are rife with trials and errors, highs and lows, rights and numerous wrongs. Yet, on the other hand, despite the frequent missteps, we are so important to our creator that he came up with something to atone for those many bad parts that are mixed in with the good.

That is where the sacrificial system first began. Animals were killed on altars, with their blood presented as an offering to cover our sins. This practice went on for thousands of years until one day, a final sacrifice was made by the one who created this sacrificial system. That sacrifice was Jesus Christ, and his blood was the ultimate key to forgiveness for all our transgressions, for all eternity.

If it were not for the sacrifice of Christ's body, the truth is we would still all spend our days constantly spilling the blood of animals on an altar, never quite managing to atone for the many mistakes and booboos we make throughout our existence.

There once lived a man who made it his mission in life to find and kill Jews in cold blood. In fact, he spent his days hunting them down, finding them in their hiding places, seeking them out one by one and dragging them off, men and women both, to jail or to their deaths. Neighbors would flood out of their houses to curse at these Jews as they were led down the streets that they and their families before them had lived and grown up on, all while this man believed he was fulfilling an important mission—to stamp out heretics and religious vermin.

This man wasn't a Nazi. In fact, he lived almost two thousand years before anyone had even heard the name of Adolf Hitler. No, this man was a devout Jew himself who went by the name of Saul.

One day, Saul was on his way to a city in the Middle East called Damascus to imprison some Jews when he was blinded by a great light. The Jews Saul was persecuting were Jews who believed in and followed Jesus as the Messiah. They were known as Christians, and Saul, who hunted them vigorously, was felled to the floor by a blinding light on this particular trip in the most spectacularly dramatic come-to-Jesus moment. Saul went on to become Paul the apostle, one of the most inspirational Christian figures in the Bible.

Saul spent several days blinded by the light he had seen, the words of Jesus echoing in his head, sent down from heaven, demanding to know from Saul why he was persecuting his followers. So Saul sat there unable to eat or drink, until a man named Ananais was instructed to go to meet him, and though he was fearful based on Saul's reputation, he did as instructed.

Now Peter, in the very few years between Christ's resurrection and the blinding of Saul, stated that everyone should "repent and be baptized . . . in the name of Jesus Christ for the forgiveness of your sins." (Acts 2:38). So Ananais baptized Saul, and all of the murderous and hateful actions Saul had committed were henceforth forgiven.

Now, each of us comes with a host of stuff that we carry through life based on the actions we have taken over the arc of our existence. Every single one of us has done things we regret, has made mistakes, been less than perfect. We may not all have gone out and imprisoned and murdered people, yet even still, goats, bulls, doves would have had to have been killed in order to atone for the mistakes we do make. Worse, that atonement would not have been permanent and all encompassing, so we would have had to have keep killing and spilling blood all the days of our lives.

The wonderful and freeing thing about Christianity is that once you become a child of God, you are forgiven for all of those mistakes, actions, and errors of judgment. Forgiveness is extended to all, even those who have perpetrated the most heinous of crimes.

Let me clarify though for a minute, for anyone who might be led to think that in a Christian book written by a gay man who does drag, the message implied here is that one needs to be forgiven for being LGBTQ+. One does not need forgiveness for being born blond, blind, or bisexual.

One needs forgiveness for the actions they take, the darkness that creeps into one's heart when they seek to tear down and destroy others by words or deeds. Forgiveness is for envy, for greed, for being obtuse or hostile toward widows and orphans or anyone else weak and in need.

With that in mind, if Saul, who was thereafter and forevermore known as the apostle Paul, could be forgiven, then absolutely anyone who walks this earth can be forgiven as well.

I have had to forgive myself for many things over throughout the years. For one, I had to forgive myself for being in relationships with women in whom I had practically no interest beyond friendship. There was one who I did remain friends with. She loved to do things in bed that involved peanut butter. I have had to make peace with the fact that I allowed one of my favorite snacks to be tarnished forever. Alas, it's a light forgiveness compared to other things.

All people test numerous relationships and situations until they find the one that works best for them. Still, a lot of straight women are downright mean when it comes to men who date them eventually coming out as gay or bisexual. Meanwhile, a lot of relationships fail, so I'm never quite comfortable with placing particular blame on the men in these relationships. Sometimes something works between men and women, women and men, men and men, etc., and other times it does not. I do wish that I had not been as confused as I was at the time, but hey, that's part of growing up. So I forgive myself for my youth and silliness.

Embrace the forgiveness that is granted by God, and do not ever look back on your past errors, except when it is fruitful to help others. Give thanks that we are made new because Jesus made the ultimate sacrifice for all of us. God has already forgiven us once we become Christians, and we need to do the same without constantly yanking back the grace we have been offered and attempting to negate the power of the cross.

PRAYER

Father in heaven, forgive me for all the things I have done wrong. My human actions, thoughts, and deeds are indeed all forgiven because of the one and true sacrifice that Jesus made on my behalf. Help me to embrace this forgiveness and know that it is eternal, just as your love for me is eternal.

REFLECTION

1. What point(s) in this chapter resonated with me the most? Why?

2. How do I demonstrate in my life that I have embraced forgiveness from God through Jesus? Are there ways I can do that more, ways that are authentic to who I am as a person?

Forgiveness for Others

"Do not judge and you will not be judged. Do not condemn and you will not be condemned. Forgive and you will be forgiven."

—LUKE 6:37

Forgiveness is not just something we receive. Instead, it is something we are contractually obligated, if you will, to pass on to others.

There is something many would call weird about me. It's that I don't hold onto any grudges or ill feelings toward people based on their prior actions. I've had many things done to me over the years, especially as a gay man. Growing up, I was horribly bullied. I've watched in horror as people did terrible things to both me and others, and yet, I would still break bread with more or less any one of those people today.

Several years ago, I wrote a piece for the Huffington Post in which I shared an incident that happened to me while I was attending a conservative Christian university in the American South, where I was studying the Bible.

Before I get into the incident, I would like to point out that so many wonderful people have attended this university. While I have strong feelings about the policies and viewpoints the university espouses and subjects people to, I want to note that numerous kind and gentle souls, who mean well and are trying their best to find their way through their own lives, are counted among the school's alumni.

On this particular day, as I walked across the campus of this Christian university, a group of guys pushed me to the ground and shouted at me that I was going to hell because I was a "faggot."

As I stated in the Huffington Post, "I was mortified . . . because I was shocked that at a place supposedly full of Christian love and fellowship, such vile hatred was present."

While my purpose at the time of writing the article was to demonstrate a key step in my journey toward self-acceptance, I highlight the story here for a completely different reason. As I lifted myself up from the ground once those buttmunches moved on, I found the fitful start of self-love. Yet it also deepened my love for those who decided on their own that they were my enemies.

This wasn't instant, mind you, but over time, I moved from feeling embarrassed, to sad, to pissed off, to freeing myself from their act of darkness.

When Jesus was on the cross dying from crucifixion, he cried out for God the Father to forgive the people killing him. Now, to keep it as real as possible, if Jesus the Son of God, and also God himself, could forgive the very people who killed him, who in the heck am I to not forgive some twits who pushed me onto the grass out of stupidity and ignorance?

In many ways, I actually pity them for being that closed-minded and thinking God is so small that he would condone being mean to others because of their differences. For that, I cannot help but forgive, and leave it to God for any judgment or retribution for people's moron-ism.

A couple of years after I graduated from the Christian university, I had fully come out, although that was a journey in itself. Up until that point, I had kept in touch on and off with a few different people from the school who were important in my life and whom I was close to. However, one by one they dropped off, citing my homosexuality as a barrier to their love, friendship, grace, etc. People I had prayed with, laughed with, wept with now saw me as an outcast.

It would have been very easy for me to be bitter about their rejection in those moments, and to remain so many years later. Instead, over time, in my heart I offered them the same forgiveness I know God gives to me, because frankly, human beings often just get it wrong. I am sure I also have done things that caused people hurt, whether consciously or subconsciously, because I too am one of those imperfect human beings.

Today, I am at a place where I would gladly sit and pray and weep and laugh with any of those self-removed friends in an instant. Not because either of us needs the other, but because Jesus said it best in Matthew 6: "For if you forgive other people when they sin against you, your heavenly

Father will also forgive you. But if you do not forgive others their sins, your Father will not forgive your sins."

Forgiveness is a two-way street in our heart, and we own a toll booth at one end. We can stay closed up on our side, a lonely, broken-down section of road in need of repair, gnarled with weeds from lack of use. Or, we can open up the gates and allow the free flow of traffic and life to carry on, with all its potholes—plus the blooming wildflowers and mountain views outside of the car windows.

There lived a king once who was calling in his debts. One man owed him thousands of bags of gold. When the man came to the throne room of the king, he confessed that he didn't have the money to pay the king back. The king demanded the man be thrown into jail. However, the man threw himself on the ground and cried for mercy. This act resonated within the king's heart, so he forgave the man his debt in its entirety.

A short time later, the newly debt-free man passed by a palace servant who owed him a handful of silver coins. The man grabbed the servant by the neck and screamed in his face that he better pay his debt to him immediately. When the servant confessed that he didn't have the money, the man threw him in prison to be tortured.

The king found out what the man whose large debt he had just forgiven had done to the servant, so he summoned him back before his throne. Furious, he berated the man for requiring the servant to pay back the small debt when the king had just forgiven the man's much larger debt.

The king called out for his guards, who dragged the man off to prison, where he was mercilessly tortured until he could repay the thousands of bags of gold for the original debt, which the king had now reinstated.

This story, told by Jesus in the book of Matthew, closes with a simple truth. "This is how my heavenly Father will treat each of you unless you forgive your brother or sister from your heart."

We are left with minimal choices in life when it comes to forgiving others, including those who are closest to us, such as family and friends. One, we can walk around in a state of hurt, anger, and chronic victimization. Or two, we can forgive others because we know that along the way, we are all in need of God's forgiveness. Plus, we can't ever move on and focus on our own development if we are looking backward or sideways at the doings of other people.

This does not mean one should run out there to get stomped on, nor that there is no accountability for terrible actions. It does mean, though, that we recognize that sometimes people do fucked up things. Pardon my language—blame the drag queen in me. It's true, though; we all step in the doodie more than once in life.

We get annoyed and lash out, we road-rage, we hold implicit biases that impact how we treat people, and we cannot even see or recognize these things. We are young and make mistakes that may make us cringe as we get older. But whatever path we walk, we all wind up in the same position, in need of the overwhelming compassion and forgiveness that God grants us. Let us then in turn do the same for others who are following the same twisting and winding road.

West Virginia Senator Robert Byrd entered the public arena organizing for his local Ku Klux Klan chapter. He spent the rest of his life apologizing for his involvement with the hate group and trying to advocate for equality. I have no doubt whatsoever that God forgave Senator Byrd, as he does all of his followers. We might not have spent any time advocating for the destruction of the lives of others like Senator Byrd did while in the Klan, and the way many of the conservative political followers who claim the mantle of Christ still do in the United States. Yet they need our forgiveness nonetheless for their deeds, however destructive those deeds might be.

That doesn't mean I won't call them out big time on their crap, of course. Ultimately, though, I lay them before God's throne.

Why? The same reason as before. Jesus forgave those whose hands had his own blood on them. God has shown us great mercy and forgiven even the worst of offenders. That is the strongest of reasons. It frees our hearts and souls from the heavy burden of hate.

Also, when and if God decides to handle those offenders in whatever way he decides, trust and believe that whatever we cook up will pale in comparison.

Shake the dust off your feet and leave the haters to their ways. God has you; God has forgiven you. Do the same to them, and keep it moving. You will find peace and freedom in that act of forgiveness.

PRAYER

God, grant me the strength to forgive others for their actions and mistakes the way you forgive me for mine. No human beyond Jesus is perfect and sinless. May I offer grace to other people on their journeys through this life.

Lord, help me to be slower to write others off or cancel them, and quicker to forgive.

REFLECTION

1. Are there people in my life I need to forgive for what they have done to either me or others? Who are they, and what do I need to forgive them for?

2. Create a special prayer where you lift each of these people up to God. Release them, and release yourself from the burden of holding on to past hurts.

Forgiveness of Self

"For all have sinned and fall short of the glory of God, and all are justified freely by His grace through the redemption that came by Christ Jesus."

—Romans 8:23–24

The last, and arguably most difficult, part of forgiveness is the kind you give to yourself. We can let go of things others do to us or walk away from those people, closing them out of our lives.

We can accept the initial big picture that God forgives us through Jesus and gives us freedom. But beyond that wide view, we have incredible difficulty releasing ourselves from the shackles of our mistakes, even though God already has. We know they are gone, but we don't allow ourselves to truly believe it deep within, so we harbor these past transgressions, bringing them back out to flay ourselves with unnecessary guilt at various times in our lives.

When I attended that Christian university, there was an enormous amount of pressure for everyone there to find marriage partners. One was not really complete without that sanctioned marriage to a member of the opposite sex, and they reminded you of that at every turn. Marriage was the only thing that could complete your Christian circle.

Frankly, I never found girls sexually attractive. Heaven knows that if anyone tried, I did. I had girlfriends—wonderful people whom I admired. If I absolutely had to be with a female, as they told me over and over and over again I must, these were great women with admirable qualities. So I took our friendships to the next level. Some were sexual, though it was honestly forced on my part. One girlfriend at that school constantly wanted to fuck around. It churned my stomach, and I tried to come up with every excuse to avoid doing anything sexual, but she had let me know that some people were saying I was gay, so I felt like had to prove otherwise. I was so confused at the time. I felt trapped, that if I did not have relations, somehow I would become exposed officially as homosexual. And gay people were expelled or forced into conversion therapy, so I just sucked it up. I shudder today at the thought—no offense, ladies! (kissy face emoji). I was trying desperately to be a straight man.

I do not hold on to these things in my mind in any negative manner toward her today, though, nor toward anyone else, including myself, because honestly, all youth experiment and have varied sexual and relational experiences. At the end of the day, it only confirmed what I didn't like, and I wound up perfectly fine as a human. In our youth, we all shake our naked asses in front of and alongside many straight, bi, and gay men and women, all in mutual silliness. Hormones rage when one is growing up, and with those hormones, penises, vaginas, and big bootie bottoms have a way of being flashed out and about into the wind. That's just a part of life. We do not operate in bubbles, and these experiences shape us.

However, faced with the heavy weight of trying to become a straight man, each night I would go to bed and pray the same thing to God. "Please Lord, lift this deviant spirit from me." Each morning, I would wake up the same person.

While others might repent of having any form of heterosexual intercourse at the marriage factory university, I repented that I did not like it and how it further confirmed my complete distaste for anything sexual with women. What was wrong with me?

No matter how many times I prayed, no matter how many times the people around me told me that gay people only go to hell, no matter how much I begged, pleaded, studied, cried, and atoned, I was still the person I was created to be. A gay man who was also a Christian.

I spent lots of time dwelling on a passage in 2 Corinthians. In it, Paul shares how he is afflicted with a thorn in his side that he repeatedly asks God to remove. God answers Paul, "My grace is sufficient for you, for my power is made perfect in weakness."

For years, I took that to mean that being gay was the thorn I was handed. It was the weakness inside of me that I was meant to overcome. So, plagued with never-ending guilt for my feelings, I pressed on, attempting to be someone I was not. I mean, sure, one can dye their hair from gray to blond, but the gray is still there at the roots. I got engaged twice to women, but engagement even to nice people did not change the roots of my being. I was born gay, as I was born with blue eyes.

Wisdom comes with maturity. When we are younger, we sometimes refuse to see the signs or follow the road laid out before us, and this is especially true when we are impressionable, when others are in our ear.

Hours before I became engaged the first time, I sat in my dorm room, sick to my stomach. I really did not want to go through with it on any level, but that was the expectation. There was the force of an unstoppable train at the Christian college to marry at all costs, and I felt it weigh on me to the point that it was hard to breathe at times. Right before I left my room to go get engaged, I prayed fervently for God to rescue me from something I felt trapped into doing.

The next part is incredibly spooky.

I said to God, *Please show me a sign if I should not go through with this engagement*, and made it clear that I would be fine if I found a way out.

On the top of a bureau, next to my bed, I had a rectangular picture frame made of very thick plastic. Now, the picture frame was about six feet off the ground and a few feet away from me, and its cube was about half an inch thick—basically one of those cheap, indestructible blocks of plastic.

The exact second the words left my lips, the frame cracked loudly. A giant piece on the side broke off and lay there on the bureau while the rest of the cube of plastic fell loudly to the floor at my feet.

It absolutely terrified me. I literally screamed so loud that a neighbor, who was incidentally this super-hot guy from West Virginia who was studying to be a minister, and always made a special point of taking care of me, ran in to check on me.

I got myself together and then went out and got engaged anyway like a great big dummy. Meanwhile, I probably could have been a preacher's wife in West Virginia to this very day if I had followed my true path and not the path the indescribable pressure of religious conformity repeatedly forced me onto.

That relationship eventually imploded, and I escaped, amen! Unfortunately, while I might have gotten away from that relationship, because of the enormity of force that the cult lays upon its adherents, it wasn't long before I was engaged again. This time, though, she really was a funny, smart, great person. We gave it a go, but it just wasn't meant to be for either of us. In the end, for both of our sakes, we parted ways. I am more than confident that she found a much happier life than the one we would have had, so I lift her up to God to continue to bless her according to his goodness and will.

As I reached the end of my time at that university, I began to feel I could no longer box myself in, nevertheless God. What if the weakness was not my being gay, but my inability to accept who God had made me? What if the power he was demonstrating was not the weakness of my sexuality changing, but instead the force was his loving me as he created me, in spite of what others might say? It would hardly be the first time God had worked through those the religious world said were outcasts or weak.

Lots of prayer, internal debate, and frankly some wisdom that comes with aging eventually led me to a place of forgiveness. This forgiveness was of myself.

I released myself from the chronic weight of guilt for something I could not and was never meant to change. I had spent wasteful, horrible years self-flagellating instead of embracing the beautiful care God took in my design. I forgave myself for being weak by allowing others to tell me I was wrong simply for being who I was meant to be, and for believing them.

Being gay had nothing to do with whether or not I could be a follower of Jesus. Being a Christian meant loving others because God loved me, and loving myself for his handiwork. Who I slept with or got married to was so low on the totem pole. How I cared for the weak, proclaimed his name, showed humility, praised him in all things—these were far more important. How dare I not accept that!

I am almost certain some readers will go off in an online review somewhere to list every sin known to mankind and place homosexuality at the top. They will insist I am going to hell for my words. What can one say to those who believe that they themselves are God? I leave these people and these matters in his hands. And I release myself from all of the guilt and self-hatred because of what people who have never walked a day in my skin would like to tell me. They really do not know the power of my Lord.

Forgiveness for oneself and letting go of your past mistakes and sins is a critical part of being a Christian. Going backward to anguish over things that God himself has forgiven and forgotten defeats the purpose of the forgiveness that is central to our faith.

PRAYER

Heavenly Father, you have already forgiven me through your Son, Jesus Christ. Help me to continually accept that forgiveness and not live in a space that looks backward. Help me not try to take back the power of the cross but to live with the knowledge that I am new to you each moment of each day through the sacrifice of your Son.

REFLECTION

1. What mistakes in my life do I revisit? Are there particular times or things that trigger me to go back to these events?

2. How can I give these over to God for good?

3. Visualize a stack of papers that contain each of the sins and mistakes you've made in the past listed within. See you handing those papers off to God and him tossing them into a fiery pit where they go up in flames. Release yourself from these forever, as they are no longer in your possession or in God's sight. Amen!

Peace with Others

"If it is possible, as far as it depends on you, live at peace with everyone."
—ROMANS 12:18

As a member of the LGTBQ+ community who is constantly under attack, coupled inherently with my disposition as a New Yorker, I must confess I find it difficult to bite my tongue in the face of injustice of any kind. Also, there are two sides always at war within me, and I assume most other people as well. One Jeza is happy-go-lucky, forgives, and lets it go. The other will cut a bitch.

I sat down on an Amtrak train a couple of years back that was heading from New York City to Toronto. A young Black man in his late teens sat in front of me, and a white, older male/female couple sat in the seats directly to his left.

Prior to the train pulling out of the station, the conductor announced, like they always do on these trains, that it would be helpful if passengers with bags put them in the overhead bins so that all seats were open and available for new passengers that the train would pick up at stops along the way.

If you have ever ridden the train from NYC to anywhere, you will know that most people ignore this announcement at first, and leave small bags on the empty seat next to them, in hopes that as people board the train, they'll move on down the line to find another open seat. In this manner, many people wind up having both seats to themselves.

The teenager had a small gym bag on the seat next to him, just like I had a computer bag on the seat next to me. Again, common practice, nothing to see here.

33

The train heaved and pulled out of Penn Station.

We couldn't have been riding more than three minutes when all of a sudden, the older white male, likely in his late sixties, literally leapt out of his seat, took the two steps across the aisle to where the young Black man was sitting, leaned into his face, and began screaming and cursing at him.

"You better move your fucking bag, because other people want to sit in this seat!"

The kid explained very nicely that he would be happy to move the bag if someone came over and needed the seat.

The older man leaned in closer, lowered his voice a notch, and as spittle flew out his mouth, cussed the kid out again, calling him names.

In today's world, one never really knows where something is headed. They tell you to mind your business, but I have a terrible time standing back when hatred is moving full speed toward someone right in front of me.

Without a second thought, I barked at the old man to leave that kid alone. Of course, I wasn't exactly the epitome of peace, as I leveled the man for treating the kid way he had and furthermore asked for his Amtrak credentials, as he obviously must work for the transportation company since he had so nastily and physically involved himself in something that would otherwise be none of his business.

What made matters worse was the old man then summoned a real Amtrak worker over, who instantly took the old man's side, without any knowledge of what had happened. Talk about implicit bias and profiling at its finest.

Needless to say, I went mental on him too.

Both myself and the young man were threatened with expulsion from the train, though we were not the perpetrators of the event in any way, shape, or form.

Things remained tense until we pulled into the train station of the location many of the passengers were going.

When all of us exited the train—the young man, the older couple, and myself—the teen was met by a big and strapping father, who looked like he could have snapped all of us in two without so much as needing to inhale.

I walked along as the kid explained to his father what happened and I offered to assist in filing a complaint against the train conductor given the terrible response, as honestly the old man should have been booted from the train, instead of the conductor threatening this guy and myself.

I'll never forget what the father's response was. He took his son's bag in his hands and started to walk away, very softly and sincerely saying, "We will pray for him." I could hear his voice fading as they exited the station. "You never know what someone else is going through. That kind of hate and anger is not about you . . ."

Dad could have gone up and pummeled the guy. He could have gone straight to the Amtrak office and demanded justice. Instead, the kid's father offered prayers and an off-ramp for what might have escalated with anyone else.

As far as it depends on you, though it is not always easy by any stretch of imagination, be at peace with others. This isn't a reboot of forgiveness, though it is related. Instead, peace is often a choice. One can make the temperature rise, take things to the next level as it were, and sometimes, as denoted in this verse, you really are left with no choice. But, when the choice is there, it is ultimately in your best interest to live in peace with others.

I worked with someone once who absolutely hated me for reasons that were not my own. They were bitter because I had received a well-earned promotion at a job. Up until this point, the person had been nice to me, but once I was promoted, they couldn't stand to look at my face. At the time, I could have easily laid into a power play, been rude back, or let everyone else know what a bitch this worker was. Instead, I prayed regularly for them.

There is another verse in Romans that says, "If your enemy is hungry, feed him. If he is thirsty, give him something to drink. For in so doing you will be heaping fiery coals on his head." As much as possible, and believe me I am saying again it is not always easy, I try to live at peace even with those who wish me harm. I lift them up in prayer and leave them at God's doorstep. He has the power to change hearts or wreak vengeance, so I must leave him to that power and lead with love.

Anyone who knows me would hardly call me a doormat, possibly the other way around. But if they truly know me, they would also know I go out of my way to try to find an entry point, a place where we can find common ground. I will not stand down on what is important, but I also know that absolutely anyone I am dealing with has a soul, has a family, etc. Thus, I try to find the human aspect over which we can meet midway. It doesn't always work, but it is always worth trying to find that common space first.

Stand up, stand firm, but lead with love and be at peace. Pray for your enemies. Peace in your soul is a gift granted to you. Take full advantage of this priceless gift.

PRAYER

It is not easy to be at peace with others, Lord, especially when they point their slings and arrows at us. My natural instinct is to stand up, and I know you understand when I need to do so. Help me though, Father, to live in peace with others. To pray for my enemies, those who wish me harm. Many of these people do not even know me, but hate me simply for being who I am. I pray for these people, Lord, and I pray your love overtakes them. I pray I take hold of the peace in my heart that you have offered me.

REFLECTION

1. Think of a recent time where you could have handled something different, in a more peaceful manner. What specifically would you have done differently? Do you think the outcome would have changed, and in what way(s)?

2. Where in your life do you struggle to be at peace with others? What are your trigger points? Where can God fit into how you manage these times?

Inner Peace

"And the peace of God, which transcends all understanding, will guard your hearts and your minds in Christ Jesus."

—PHILIPPIANS 4:7

There is probably nothing more important to one's psyche than inner peace. You cannot function at your fullest without being at peace within your own being. When you strip all the external away, peace is something that fills up your headspace, and your headspace alone. However, you are not in there by yourself, actually. One of the greatest benefits to having a relationship with God is that he is in those private spaces with you, and this fact is where the true basis of peace begins and ends.

I had recently moved to Los Angeles after college when I walked into a local bank to open a checking account.

The moment I entered, a clerk ushered me to her desk near the entrance. The chair I sat in opposite her left me with my back facing the bank's door and a large wall of windows that looked out into the parking lot.

Within seconds of me sitting down, the woman who was assisting me in opening my account suddenly looked up from the paperwork we were filling out together. Her eyes widened, and they looked right past me. She exhaled a loud gasp of terror and stopped speaking.

I turned around to find the barrel of a gun pointed directly in my face.

In a nanosecond, an inexplicable peace passed through my body. It was not just mental peace, but a physical feeling that had washed over me. In that moment, in the "knowing" part of my mind or soul (not sure where it is housed, to be fair), I could hear something inform me that I was safe and that this was not the day I was to die.

Screams echoed throughout the rest of the bank as three other gunmen corralled customers to the middle of the lobby. My bandit motioned for us to do the same. He guided me at gunpoint to lie down on the lobby floor with the others.

Once we were all on the ground, two robbers stayed with us, while one ran to the bank tellers at the counter and ordered them to empty their drawers. The fourth gunman forced one of the employees to walk with him into the bank's vault.

Time seemed to stand still. The people on the floor around me were sobbing and shaking.

Finally, the one who went into the vault emerged with bags that appeared to be full. In moments, all the thieves had backed their way out of the bank and fled.

I looked around to tear-soaked faces. It hit me that I just had a gun literally in my face but that I had not one drop of panic or concern in my body. I knew I was not going to die. Not for one second did I think I was in danger.

Perhaps it was knowing that I was saved and would live on whether my physical body ceased to operate or not that led me to feel that way. Perhaps it was what doubters would call the anti- scientific connection that God exists in me.

Personally, I know I do not have to define it for anyone. God is, and he imparts his peace to those who call on him.

The letter to the Philippians makes it perfectly clear that there exists a peace, a knowing, that goes way beyond the capacity for humans to understand, nevertheless explain. The ultimate peace is recognizing that I do not have to.

Later in my life, I have developed a strange sleep anxiety that terribly grips me on occasion. On these nights, if I do not fall asleep within minutes of lying down, I get incredibly overwhelmed by stress. This tension pours adrenaline into my body, which in turn further stops me from falling asleep. A miserable cycle sets in where I become completely worked up, and it can last for hours, especially when I know I have to be up early to go somewhere.

In order to break myself out of these cycles, I have found one of the most effective things I can do is to talk to God and lean into those powerful verses of the Bible that can cover over and cancel out my sleep anxiety to give me inner peace.

I find it difficult to describe to people the way I feel when I have these episodes. It feels like I'm mentally drowning, like I'm gasping for air. Sometimes, it can be quite physical. When I'm hit with these moments, though, I become amazed by how fragile we are as people. We can seemingly have it together one minute, then turn into complete nutburgers the next.

However, while I find it hard to explain to people the feelings that this sleep anxiety evokes in me, I know that I've been promised a powerful peace that goes beyond my own limited comprehension. A peace so powerful, it has the ability to consume my mere mortal disquiet and those feelings of insurmountable stress.

When life is at its lowest points for me. When I am the most stressed out that I can ever be. When I doubt myself. When I feel fear. When I am crushed by pain, or fall into a panic over things I cannot put to words.

In those moments, I hold on to and dive headfirst into that deep inner peace that is inexplicable even to myself. I embrace the fact that God and his love for me surpass anything and everything that I feel, including my piddling anxiety, which is ultimately so small in the scheme of the world and his great plan.

One verse I lean on in difficult times is Isaiah 26:3: "You will keep in perfect peace those whose minds are steadfast, because they trust in you." There is a beautiful hymn that was written by an English Bishop, Edward H. Bickerseth, during the 1800s based on this verse in Isaiah. It was said to be a favorite of another queen, named Victoria.

When I cannot fall asleep, I repeat the song over and over in my mind until I feel the peace wash over me. It has a lulling melody, so feel free to look it up and make it a part of your own inner calming repertoire.

> *Peace, perfect peace, in this dark world of sin?*
> *The blood of Jesus whispers peace within.*
> *Peace, perfect peace, by thronging duties pressed?*
> *To do the will of Jesus, this is rest.*
> *Peace, perfect peace, with sorrows surging round?*
> *On Jesus's bosom naught but calm is found.*
> *Peace, perfect peace, with loved ones far away?*
> *In Jesus's keeping we are safe, and they.*
> *Peace, perfect peace, our future all unknown?*
> *Jesus we know, and He is on the throne.*

Jesus says a sparrow does not fall without the Father knowing. My anxiety is but a tiny bit of dander on a sparrow's tail feather, so God can easily handle it.

There is a peace that passes our human ability to comprehend, a peace that comes from a relationship with God. It is something impossible to articulate or explain fully to others, yet it exists.

Let that peace drift into the far and hidden spaces of your being that only you and the one who created you can enter. In those spaces, feel the presence of the Almighty and breathe in the deep peace that goes way beyond any of your worries or concerns. Let it consume your heart and mind.

PRAYER

Father, when I feel lost in my own worries and emotions, let me lean into your peace. Although the peace you are able to bring is something that others, or even I, cannot ever fully understand, your peace transcends my heart, my mind, and all things. You are bigger than anything and everything. Let me rest in this peace that comes from knowing and loving you. Help me fall into your peace like a soft pillow.

REFLECTION

1. What does the Philippians passage say to me about inner peace in my life?

2. What verses, songs, prayers, and forms of meditation can I place in a spiritual toolbox to call upon in times of need?

Allies

*"Speak up for those who cannot speak for themselves,
for the rights of all who are destitute."*

—PROVERBS 31:8

There is a major group who often get overlooked when it comes to the LG-BTQ+ community. These people are not themselves Lesbian, Gay, Bisexual, Transgender, Queer, Intersex, Asexual, or any other variation of identification. However, without them, many of the rights that our community have earned and readily enjoy today would not exist.

One day in high school, I was being picked on by a group of people while I was at my locker trying to put some books in and take other ones out. The group was teasing me and calling me names, when a young woman walked over and slammed one of the aggressors' Trapper Keeper out of his hands, sending it spilling onto the floor while she yelled out, "Leave him alone!" Everyone stopped dead in their tracks and backed away. They left me alone for the rest of the day because the young woman had allied herself with my plight.

When I was older, a female employee complained to another female employee that they didn't think I deserved my job because they didn't believe that the organization should hire anyone who was openly gay. The second employee, who was a large woman, physically stood up from her seat to cower over the complainer, looked down at her, and said, "Assholes come in every color, and yours is green with envy." She said this because I was well-liked at the job by all but this one person. My hero told the complainer to never fuck with me again, and she never did.

Allies matter.

Around the year 486 BC, King Xerxes, ruler of the Persian Empire, was about to have all the Jews in his kingdom killed at his advisor Hamman's recommendation. His Queen, Esher, had never revealed her Jewish origins to King Xerxes, and without Xerxes summoning her to his throne, she had no way to petition him to save the Jewish people's lives, lest she herself be put to death for entering his throne room without an invitation.

Putting her own life at risk, she approached the king, and in doing so eventually saved all of the Jews living in Persia at that time.

Esther easily could have kept on living her life of luxury as queen and never lifted a pinky toe to help the Jews. Instead, she put her own neck on the line to save countless others.

This is what allies do. They stand up to bullies. They put themselves at great risk, often because they believe that right is right no matter the cost.

When I attend Pride marches and parades, drag performance, and other events that raise awareness, funds, or support for LGBTQ+ causes, I am often amazed and humbled by the sheer number of straight people who attend these events and champion our causes.

These are our neighbors, friends, family members, and work colleagues, who step out and stand up for us, sometimes in the most subtle of ways and sometimes in the loudest and proudest of ways to let us know that they have our backs.

There would be no marriage equality without the straight people in Congress who voted for it and the straight judges on the court who ruled for it. There would be no safe spaces, healthcare centers that meet our needs, marches, or laws to protect our day-to-day existence without our allies helping to make these things happen.

That is why I for one am so thankful to be living in an age where more and more churches are opening their doors to LGBTQ+ people and acknowledging their value and importance to the cause of Christ. Thank God, literally, for these brave leaders and practitioners of faith. They are beautiful and wonderful representations of the Lord.

Yes, we banged down many doors, but we never did it alone, and often there was a straight person on the other side who heard our plea, unlocked the door, turned the knob, and let us in.

In a particularly well-known story in the Bible, a woman was about to be stoned for sleeping with men. The mob surrounded her, ready to pounce. Encircled, humiliated, and fearing for her life she was at the mercy of the crowd. A man who was present stood up before those with the rocks in their hands that they planned to use to bash the woman's brains in with. He stood tall and said, "Let anyone who is without sin be the first to throw a stone at her" (John 8:7). One by one, the men dropped the rocks at their feet and left.

Jesus stood up for this woman, though the aim of the mob was to condemn not just her, but him as well.

There is no greater ally than God. Over and over again, scripture makes it abundantly clear that God stands with those whom the masses do not. He does not ask or implore us, but instead repeatedly he commands us to be the one who counters the bully, the one who rises tall for the weak, to be the person who ensures that there is justice for the marginalized and anyone in a weaker and less equal position. He is the ultimate champion of equity and equality. In fact, our God is the very definition of woke.

Thank heavens for those who follow his command and his lead and stand up for and alongside us in our never-ending fight for equal treatment as beautiful beings that God himself created.

Change does not just happen solely from those on the outside looking in. It also comes from those on the inside who take action at all costs.

PRAYER

Lord in heaven, thank you for those who advocate for the LGBTQ+ community. They are not just friends and family, they are allies. Please bless them for putting themselves out there on our behalf and for fighting alongside us for basic human decency. Thank you, Lord, for being our ultimate advocate. You created us and love us with all the colors of the rainbow we possess in our souls.

REFLECTION

1. Who are the people in your life who have been your allies? What actions did they take?

2. How can you show appreciation for the allies who step out with you, even if their support is shown in gentle ways?

3. In what areas and ways can you be a better ally to others?

Humor and Laughter

"This is the day the Lord has made; let us rejoice and be glad in it."
—PSALMS 118:24 (KJV)

There is a perception that God is a gigantic bore and that anyone practicing Christianity should consistently walk around with a face like a slapped arse. What a miserable point of view!

The Bible is filled with quotes about joy and laughter. A favorite of mine reads, "A cheerful heart is a good medicine, but a downcast spirit dries up the bones." (Proverbs 17:22). I would be unable to list all of the moments in my life when laughter lifted my spirit, even in times of distress and tribulation. Equally, I could not list the times when being downcast and miserable led me even further into the abyss.

When my partner was admitted to the hospital with an undiagnosed, life-threatening medical emergency, I had an opportunity after many hours at this bedside to return to our apartment for a quick shower and to get a change of clothes. We had been in the ER for over sixteen hours, and he had finally been admitted and placed in a private room. This was my first chance to run back, charge my phone, and eat something. I grabbed both his and my belongings and ran out the door.

About an hour later, I returned to the hospital and approached the security desk. This hospital required you to present identification and go through a metal detector upon entrance.

I reached into my wallet and handed the security officer my driver's license while I signed in on the paper provided. The security officer looked at my license and looked back at me with a funny face.

I should tell you that in New York State, the picture on your license can be automatically reused over the course of many years. In my case, when I first had this particular photo taken for my license, I was significantly younger—so much so that I had a full head of hair. The boy-me of today when out of drag does not even have one lonely lock left on his shiny bald head. On top of that, when I took the photo, I was a twig who weighed a pound and a half wet. At present, each of my toes individually could balance the scales with the boy in the license photo.

With those two things in mind, I explained to the officer that the person in the photo was me, it was just a very old photograph.

This explanation did not sit well with him. He looked at the photo again and then back at me, giving me an accusatory glare.

Now, I have to put things into perspective before I go on. I'd come home less than twenty-four hours before after a full day's work to a husband who looked like death warmed over. We rushed to the ER, then spent the night and into the next day not knowing if he was living or dying and of what. I briefly ran home for an hour and had basically not slept at this point in a day and a half, but I was still standing based on pure worry and adrenaline. Someone glaring at me over my old license picture was the last straw for my already regularly thin New York patience. All I wanted to do was to get back upstairs and make sure my partner was alive.

"Look," I said to the man, "it's an old picture, but it's obviously me. You can see we have the exact same eyes!"

The officer informed me that he would need to contact his supervisor. I rolled my eyes in pure annoyance as he signaled for another officer to come over.

He handed the supervisor my identification. This man looked back and forth from the license to me three or four times.

I lost my shit.

"Listen, I have been up for thirty-six-plus hours. The photo is me. You know New York just reuses the same license photo over and over again."

He looked skeptical.

"I have the same eyes, I'm just a lot older, I now have no hair, and I got fat!" I yelled. I was really pissed off now.

The supervisor officer said, "You are telling me this is you?"

I went completely mental. I screamed, "Yes, it's me! It's the same face, just older! I haven't changed *that* much!"

The security man then said, "If you are telling me this is your face, then we have got a major problem."

He turned the license around, and I found myself staring at my partner's photograph. Mind you, I am a white man, while my partner is Black.

It was only a nanosecond before I burst into absolute hysterical laughter.

I explained to the officer that this was my partner's license. When I grabbed his belongings before I left the hospital to shower, I must have placed his ID into my wallet next to my own. When I returned to the hospital, I pulled out the wrong license, which I handed the security guard.

All three of us heaved with laughter. The supervisor chuckled that when I'd said I hadn't changed that much, he thought changing from white skin to black skin was a pretty significant physical transformation.

Those few moments of cackling released almost two days of intense worry and stress. Instantly, I felt like a completely different person, one who had been brought back to life.

Laughter really is such great medicine.

My mother, and hence the rest of my immediate family, converted from Judaism to become members of the super-conservative Church of Christ. Jews, and New York Jews at that, are anything but uptight, yet while members of the Churches of Christ have lots of good laughs themselves, they are at times so puritanical that many members could produce the finest of diamonds in their uptight, puckered holes.

They have firm beliefs that people should not dance, especially not with members of the opposite sex. One should remain chaste, and never drink; there should be no musical instruments in churches, etc. I'm not criticizing them for their beliefs, as I understand clearly why they hold many of these to be true, but the level of prudishness borders at times on *The Handmaid's Tale*. To be blunt, they are one step and a half away from "praise be."

One time I was out with a group of church members, and the conversation somehow got onto the topic of dancing. I greatly amused myself by singing aloud some modified lyrics to the musical *My Fair Lady*, where Audrey Hepburn sang, "I could have danced all night, I could have danced all night . . ." However, I revised these words and began to sing, "I could have danced all night, but I was Church of Christ . . ."

You would have thought that I'd choked someone's mamma. The people I was with became incredibly incensed at my silly song, insisting the words were sinister and ungodly.

Um, okay. I was fairly certain God was singing along with a grin to this innocent and lighthearted tune.

Today, as a drag queen, I am drawn to bawdy humor. Now, the book of Ephesians does state that Christians should avoid coarse joking. "Nor should there be obscenity, foolish talk or coarse joking" (Ephesians 5:4). However, for me, I look at the context of the whole book and passage and find Paul to be speaking about the importance of not being mean-spirited, or seeking to tear people down. Rather, we should be uplifting, and we should in all things be demonstrating the love we have received and in turn giving that love to others. Those are the kinds of things that set us apart as Christians that I believe Paul is really getting at. Our aims should center on sharing the light and love that we have through Jesus. We should be noticeable to the world because when these come from Christ, we are set apart and have a duty to spread the message to the world.

I am willing to bet that God is far less interested in my stand-up routine and its blue jokes than he is in my heart that is filled with love, joy, and thanksgiving, and the fact that I proclaim Christ as supreme. If you weigh the words in Ephesians against the whole of the Bible, tending to widows and orphans seem to outweigh a bad joke. Recognizing the sovereignty of Christ as Messiah and sharing the good news to the world by helping others find this joyous salvation might rate a notch or two above my riffing off a few "fuck yous" on stage or in print.

Throughout the Bible, good people of faith sang, danced, and drank wine. God is not an uptight overlord. I believe he wants us to be filled with joy and laughter, so long as ultimately, we remember that he is the most important thing in our lives and that all of our sins are forgiven and washed away with the acceptance of Christ, not at our own hands.

When it comes to things like crass humor, in comparison to the pharisaical American-Political- Christianity we have today, I go straight to Jesus's own words for guidance. In the book of Matthew, Jesus goes in hard on the followers of the law, who abide by every jot and tittle but miss God's intentions by a mile.

"Woe to you, teachers of the law and Pharisees, you hypocrites! You give a tenth of your spices—mint, dill and cumin. But you have neglected the more important matters of the law— justice, mercy and faithfulness. You should

have practiced the latter, without neglecting the former. You blind guides! You strain out a gnat but swallow a camel.

Woe to you, teachers of the law and Pharisees, you hypocrites! You clean the outside of the cup and dish, but inside they are full of greed and self-indulgence. Blind Pharisee! First clean the inside of the cup and dish, and then the outside also will be clean.

Woe to you, teachers of the law and Pharisees, you hypocrites! You are like whitewashed tombs, which look beautiful on the outside but on the inside are full of the bones of the dead and everything unclean. In the same way, on the outside you appear to people as righteous but on the inside you are full of hypocrisy and wickedness." (Matthew 23:23–28)

Drag humor looks positively innocent in comparison to fake religion, where we practice piety but lack love. I'll take sexual innuendo any day over hypocrisy.

As a Christian, and in your relationship with God, it is more than okay to embrace life. We should feel free to take in all of the joy that is around us in this beautiful world. We should laugh until we cry, and live each day with a cheerful heart. Laughter, joy, and cheer are all free but priceless gifts from above.

Our knowing, loving, and proclaiming God makes it so that it can be said, "Then our mouth was filled with laughter, and our tongue with shouts of joy; then they said among the nations, "The LORD has done great things for them." (Psalms 126:2 ESV)

PRAYER

Lord, you gave me humor and laughter. Let me not be afraid to use them both freely, as they are gifts. Let me feel the good medicine of laughter heal me in my bones. I thank you for all the times in my life that you fill up with joy. Father, sprinkle my life with giggles and guffaws, as they are key components to a full and rich life.

REFLECTION

1. During what times in my life has humor healed my heart or helped me through a bad situation?

2. Do I acknowledge God in moments of tear-inducing laughter or only in the hour of need?

3. How can I embrace and share the radiating freedom of laughter that has been gifted to me from above?

God's Love for You

"This is love: not that we loved God, but that he loved us and sent his Son as an atoning sacrifice for our sins."

—1 JOHN 4:10

In college, we would go on mission trips often outside of the United States. These were really wonderful experiences on many levels, with lots of singing, praying, fellowshipping, and sharing of our love for God with others.

One time, while I was in Scotland, we were missioning in a place on the eastern coast. The exact name of the city escapes me at the moment, but the memory of meeting Mark does not.

As part of our mission work, which we also called campaigning, we spent lots of time with church members who graciously housed and fed us as we spread out around the different towns, knocking on doors and performing hymns and the like in various places like public squares and nursing homes.

Mark's family—his father, mother, and brother—attended the local church in one of these small cities. Mark himself did not attend the church. In fact, he was on the outside of his family and his church because he was out and open about being a young gay man.

When I met Mark, I was instantly attracted to him. I went on numerous campaigns to the United Kingdom, and Mark was, in full transparency, the only person with whom I ever felt that feeling we get when someone ticks our boxes. For the most part, I just buried that part of me and fell full-heartedly into the life of a Chistian male attending a conservative college that aligned to one of the most conservative churches in America. Not to say I never did the normal things young men do when growing up and hormones stir; it's just that I had that butterflies-in-stomach feeling when I met Mark.

Mark's family were greatly concerned for him and convinced he was going to hell. Our mission was, of course, to save Mark from himself and Satan. With that in mind, we were introduced during what must have been a difficult time for Mark. He was living with a boyfriend who had recently beat him up.

Mark and I clicked, so I shared with him my story of salvation. As a result, Mark decided to leave his boyfriend, move back home, and be baptized.

I will never in all my life forget baptizing Mark in his bathtub, which we filled with water in between packing his stuff up from his boyfriend's apartment.

Jesus died by his own Father's plan for Mark just like he died for me. He died to atone for our sins and make us whole. I do not, nor will I ever, regret sharing that story with Mark and baptizing him into the faith.

What I do regret greatly is telling Mark that homosexuality was the sin he was guilty of and that he was not worthy of walking with Christ unless he had no feelings for or interaction with men. That he must give up this part of himself that frankly one who is born gay cannot give up any more than they can give up their blood type.

Somehow, along the way, we as humans got this idea that there is variation to sin. Like it is okay that everyone lies at times, that kids do not follow their parents' instructions, that a curse word might slip out (or pour out in my case) or an alcoholic drink may even pass one's lips from time to time. Even if we consider homosexuality to be a sin, somehow it became seen as worse than all the other things that one could be or do. Meanwhile, we are comfortable with passing widows, orphans, the homeless, and those in need on the streets of our community while turning a numb and blind eye. We give ourselves a pass on these sins but rush to judgment over the appropriate medical care of someone transitioning their physical gender. These reported sins are so much worse than anything the rest of the Christian world is doing.

It's not true, though.

The real truth is that no matter who you love—whether you're straight, gay, or bisexual—and whatever gender you are on the outside or inside, you are just a person.

Paul says it best in Romans 3:23: "For all have sinned and fallen short of the glory of God." There is no ranking. No scale that tips the level of human choices and decisions toward a better or worse weight.

God loved Mark then as a gay man just as he loved someone else as a straight man because both had fallen short of his glory for a myriad of reasons, their sexual preference being the least of them. Yet in spite of that, God's love was so perfect, and is so perfect, that he laid out the ultimate sacrifice on the altar that was so pure, it ended the need to ever sacrifice for any of us ever again.

The message I should have imparted to Mark is the same message I as a Christian continue to struggle with on a daily basis. It is not that my relationship with God is predicated on my sexuality, but rather that it is dependent upon where I place God in the pecking order of my life. This is the same for all people, gay or straight. Where God ranks is what matters most.

When the Pharisees and Sadducees got together to test Jesus, they asked him what the greatest commandment of the law was. Jesus didn't answer, "Do not have homosexual sex." Neither did he say, "If you want to use a different pronoun or choose to medically change the junk you were born with, you are burning in the fiery pits because this is so important to God." He answered, "Love the Lord your God with all your heart and with all your soul and with all your mind. This is the first and greatest commandment. And the second is like it: 'Love your neighbor as yourself.' All the Law and the Prophets hang on these two commandments." (Matthew 22:37–40).

We waste so much time in this world telling others what they should not be doing in bed. We want to police their sex lives, tell them right from wrong, legislate whether or not a man in a dress and a wig can perform within fifty feet of another breathing person. All of this is completely and utterly meaningless when put up alongside the words of Christ himself. That's what I should have said to Mark.

Love is pure and comes from God. As long as God is at the center of your being, he will fill you up. Whether you find love with another man or a woman in this world is irrelevant.

It took me some years to take those man-made shackles off my own ankles. I wish I could have known then what I know now. I would have been a much better vessel for Christ to Mark and others. I would have been a much better Christian and friend.

It is not homosexuality or your gender that stands between you and God; it never was. God's love for you is complete and threads through your being, the being that he himself created.

PRAYER

Lord, help me to embrace myself the way you have embraced me. Your love for me is full and goes down to the roots, atoms, soul, and spirit of who I am. Help me to put you first in all things. Help me to love my neighbors and to love myself, as it is sometimes hard to when those around us want us to believe we are unlovable by you. Hold my hand and let me feel your never-ending love that obliterates any words or feelings that come from anyone but you.

REFLECTION

1. What are the things that hold me back from fully accepting God's love for me?

2. In which ways have I allowed other people to hold me back from my own belief and relationship with God?

3. How can I lean on the Almighty to move beyond man's judgments and into his open arms?

Homosexuality and Relationships

"And now these three remain: faith, hope, love.
But the greatest of these is love."

—1 CORINTHIANS 13:13

Probably no topic, outside of gender conformity, will add fuel to the culture-war fires of the day the way that gay relationships do. If you want to see Karen's hair go up in smoke, have two men kiss in front of her, or better yet, ask her to bake a cake for their wedding.

Yet, for all the carrying on that takes place, Jesus himself says nothing about homosexuality, and the parts of the Bible that do presumably speak to sexuality are drenched in context both in terms of the time the particular scripture was written and in terms of the audience that was being addressed.

For example, the Old Testament verses are fairly easily explained right off the bat. In Genesis, the story of Sodom and Gomorrah was exclusively about the norms of hospitality that existed at the time, along with the horror of threatened rape. These were the reasons the cities were burned to the ground. This passage has been an easy out for those seeking to convince themselves and others that homosexuals are wicked. However, it winds up being a forest-for-the-trees scenario, as the whole point of the story comes down to: do not be a dick and do not threaten to perpetrate sexual violence against others.

The Levitical passages, along with the many other laws that we no longer blink twice at for not following, were highly timebound. To set themselves apart from the other nations, the Jews were given a strict set of laws to follow that ran counter to the ones the Gentiles of the time followed.

Specifically, pagans performed acts of homosexuality at shrines and temples before pagan gods, as acts of devotion to their idols. Therefore, God specifically forbade the Jews from doing the same.

For goodness' sake, the same exact passage in Leviticus that says do not sleep with a man as a woman or both should be killed also says you're up a creek with God if you wear clothes made from two different fibers. Cotton and wool together will spell your doom! In other words, it mattered in the broader context of "the pagans do this, so we do not."

For the New Testament verses outside of Romans, there continues to be enormous debate as to the translation choices in most of these passages. Scholars of Greek go round and round, back and forth, and upside down trying to pinpoint exactly what Paul meant in these verses, as the Greek words used do not equate directly to love between two men or two women. Some argue that the words used do not even speak to sex at all but broader traits or acts.

It is murky once we get into the weeds. What is clearer though is that much like the Old Testament verses, the passages in the New Testament must be viewed through the same lenses of time and context. At that time, our modern understanding of homosexuality did not exist.

That leads us to the biggest kicker passage in regard to homosexuality, which is Romans 1. In this letter, Paul lays out the fact that salvation through Jesus Christ is available to all people, everywhere.

Paul begins with a broad overview of history that lays out how mankind repeatedly turned God aside. As a result, he gave them over to their idolatry, their sinful nature, which is one in which any man or woman puts themselves first above God. He illustrates this through language that is again heavily debated by scholars in terms of the differing Greek translations.

The gist, though, is perfectly clear—this is not a passage about gay or lesbian sex acts, but a passage about how God is supreme, yet mankind continually elevates himself above God and thus suffers by being left to his own self-consuming demise.

If you go down to the end of the chapter, Paul lists traits that exist in every single person who has ever breathed. No one of these trumps the other. What is more fascinating to me is the nature of humans to latch on to the supposed homosexuality piece of Paul's message but completely ignore the part about lack of love and mercy with which the chapter concludes.

So basically, religious church conservatives with an agenda will rail that Romans is clear in its condemnation of homosexual acts of lust but say nothing about the lack of love or mercy with which they approach others.

When you consider Romans against the full arc of scripture, you come to see that Paul is not really addressing what we would term as homosexuality today, or gay relationships even. What he is addressing is that from day dot in the Garden of Eden, mankind has fallen prey to themselves. By trying to make ourselves equal to God and not recognizing our place, we have been a complete mess. As Romans goes on to demonstrate, there exists no greater illustration than the Israelites, who turned away over and over again. Yet, the book really makes its point in that regardless of what we do, we still have a God who loves us. One who offered up salvation and freedom from our nature through Jesus.

Nothing else, including who you love, has any bearing on this.

Almost fifteen years ago, I started chatting with someone online. After a few weeks, we agreed to meet. We approached each other outside of the Brooklyn Museum on September 22, 2009. The moment we said hello, I felt a bolt of electricity shoot from the heel of my foot, up my legs and spine to the back of my neck. It was the weirdest sensation, but as I looked in the other person's eyes, I knew instantly I had just met the man I would spend the rest of my life with.

My now husband is honestly the most amazing person one could ever be so fortunate as to find in a partner. He is loving, generous, kind, smart, and best of all, God-fearing, having literally grown up in the church, as his father is a pastor. I was so blessed to find someone who had the same contours to their own faith that I possessed in mine. That shared belief system helped, but I recognize fully how rare this is. We have laughed together, shared great moments of joy and sadness, and prayed together frequently over the years. There is not one person alive who can tell me that my relationship with my partner is not a direct blessing from God above. I know it, my partner knows it, and honestly, God knows it because we have discussed it, God and I, more times than I can count. When all is said and done, when I stand, or rather lay flat on my face, in front of God on his throne, I trust fully and completely in his judgment and mercy. I know with every inch of my being that is both body and soul that when God speaks, there is no rebuttal. Becky from Bucksnot, Arkansas can yell from here to kingdom come about her views on homosexuality. I AM reigns supreme.

My prayer for all of my gay, lesbian, bisexual, transgender, and non-conforming brothers and sisters out there is that they are as fortunate in God-given love as I am. You are not to be denied love because you came out of the womb being attracted to men or women. Rather, whomever you love, as with anything you do in life, the key is to remember who is first. Putting God first supersedes the preferred anatomy of your partner. Thinking otherwise attempts to usurp his power.

PRAYER

Heavenly Father, thank you for making me a being who has love to give and love to receive. There is peace in knowing that all love comes from you, just as your word says. You also say that love is patient and kind and that it always perseveres. Thank you, for the people in my life whom I have the honor of loving and being loved by. May I always be surrounded and filled up with love through deep, abiding, and happy relationships. I know that love is love no matter what anyone else says because you are love and you are I AM.

REFLECTION

1. Where do I see my relationship with God through the lens of sexuality?

2. How can I approach this relationship in a new way after reading this chapter?

3. What are my thoughts on God's role in my relationships?

Self-Love

"Love your neighbor as yourself."

—MATTHEW 22:39

When asked about the greatest commandment, Jesus said loving others the way we love ourselves was right near the tippy top. There is no other specific verse in the Bible that points so directly to what God knows about us—we are obsessed with ourselves!

Think about it for a second. We freely and willingly take "me time," where we do things that clear our mind and make us feel whole again. We pamper ourselves, take spa days, go on vacation, eat out at fancy restaurants, enjoy a beer on the porch. We jump up at a potluck line to get the good stuff. We rush to the front when boarding a train or an airplane. We flip refresh on our screens endlessly to get those tickets to a hot concert act before anyone else.

Jesus puts it all out there on full display in Matthew 22. What if we treated others in this same manner? What if we made sure their needs were fully met the way we do for ourselves?

About a year ago, I was in the airport in Las Vegas. My partner and I had been sitting down in a corridor, charging our phones. Just as we stood up and unplugged to get ready to board our plane, a man came running from around the corner. He screamed out, "Run!"

We, much like the rest of the airport, were shell-shocked momentarily and stood in our tracks, paralyzed by indecision. As the man ran by, in between breaths, he managed to huff out, "There's someone with a gun shooting people!"

That was enough for the dozens of people around us and our stationary bodies to get our behinds into gear and flee.

Within seconds, my partner and I were running down the opposite corridor, desperately looking for an exit or somewhere to hide.

Some people knocked others over, leaving them in the dust to suffer whatever fate awaited them. Others dragged strangers along. One man grabbed the back of a person's wheelchair and pulled them both into the men's room for cover.

We made it all the way to the end of the terminal, only to find we were shut in by the closed doors of the terminal's gates.

As we sat ducked behind one of the customer service counters, a woman who was alone behind a nearby counter was crying hysterically, repeating aloud over and over again that she wanted to go home. Mind you, this was a grown woman who was rocking back and forth in a childlike manner, in full hysteria.

Seeing her terror from a few feet away, we gently coaxed her to come hide behind the same counter as us. She mustered up the courage to move, practically leaping onto the floor between my partner and me. We let her know that she was not alone and that we would do everything in our power to protect her and each other. She cowered underneath us, crying.

It is in these moments that you truly see people's character shine through—in their actions to others.

No wonder Jesus said do to others what you would have them do to you, because when push comes to shove, our innate disposition as people is to self-preserve. Fight-or-flight is all about survival, making sure one's own body lives to see another day.

Believe me when I say, do not ever look toward me from any direction for perfection on any level. You will not find it here. Yet, I try to keep Jesus's words at the forefront of my mind in all things. It is easy to look out for ourselves, but much harder (and it goes against our grain) to look out for others in that same manner. I mean, we will do it, but usually only after we are good and taken care of.

One silly showbiz example is, I always applaud at any event I attend in the same manner I would want others to applaud for me. It does not matter if the show or act is wildly successful, totally put together, or a complete bomb. I know how hard it is to step out onto a stage. To put yourself out there under the glare and judgment of others is quite scary. Performing is exhilarating, but it is also an act of bravery that not many have the guts to try. I will literally, no matter what I see or hear, cheer for others with a glad heart. In doing so, I also feel like I fill up my own love cup— the joy of doing unto others lifts my own spirit.

What does any of this have to do with loving oneself, someone might ask? Everything.

Many modern theologians caution us about self-love, acknowledging that the American spirit is one of pure self-centeredness. In other words, it is already all about us. In our society, we love ourselves to the nth degree. The very nature of Karen behavior is predicated almost entirely on the premise of valuing oneself above others and daring anyone to disagree or cross or challenge us and our privilege.

Yet for marginalized people, especially LGBTQ+ individuals, self-love is often a critical piece that is missing in our lives. Being able to not just accept but really love ourselves can be difficult when the world around us tells us that our worth is lower than low. That we are worthless if we act a certain way, dress a certain way, or love a certain way.

Take, for example, effeminate men. In our culture, as in many others, effeminate men are often mocked, and far too often abused spiritually, mentally, and physically.

Jimmy was an especially effeminate boy who lived in my neighborhood growing up. Jimmy was a year older than me, and as such, by the time we were both in high school, we would ride the same school bus.

Day after day, kids would cruelly tease Jimmy for being effeminate. Whether it was the clothes he wore, the way he spoke, or the manner of his movements, he could barely move a muscle on or off the school bus without the constant taunting and bullying of the mob.

To my discredit, I would shrink into my seat on the bus when these events took place, because I was also often subject to the same cruelty. As I receded into the vinyl, I tried to become invisible so that I would not also be ganged up on and become a victim. On top of that, I rarely if ever spoke to Jimmy at any point during my time growing up. Any association with him scared me. How weak of me!

Looking back, though, I have come to find I have a great admiration for Jimmy, then and now. No matter what those guys and girls threw at him, he came out every day with his head held high, often as fashionable and attractive as one could possibly be, which in turn only encouraged the jerks, as they had fresh fodder beyond his mannerisms and speech.

I, on the other hand, wasn't quite as self-confident. Wherever and whenever I could, I tried to hide, blend in, and walk between the shadows.

The way Jimmy embraced himself against the onslaught of mean-girl youth wound up being something I have carried with me all these years.

Self-love for LGBTQ+ people is not about self-centeredness, it's about knowing one's worth and surviving.

You cannot ever be full or complete if you cannot recognize the beauty and be grateful for the incredible you that was created by the infinite and almighty.

Self-love for our community means understanding that God made you who you are, as colorful and as fabulous as that is. You are his creation, and if God loves you, why on earth would, could, or should you not love yourself?

PRAYER

I AM, you made me to be "just me." I can be no one else because you knew me in my womb and all of your creations are wondrous, including this one right here. Help me, my Father and friend, to love myself for every aspect of my personhood. At my deepest core, I need your assistance in finding pure contentment and then becoming elated at the me I am, no matter what anyone else has to say about it. They are unimportant. Your belief in and full support of me can topple anyone's thoughts and beliefs about my value or worth as I live my most authentic life. Help me to own myself and to love myself. In turn, Lord, help me then to go out and help others to find full and complete self-love through you, their creator.

REFLECTION

1. If I list out all of the wonderful aspects of my being, my qualities and abilities, which qualities were innate at birth and which were developed along the way? Where do I see God's hand in both the innate and the developed?

2. In what ways can I better demonstrate my love for myself?

3. How can I embrace who I am at my deepest core, including my sexuality, gender, or inability to fit into any specific identification? What is God's role in doing this both in the present and in the future?

61

Friendship

"Greater love has no one than this: to lay down one's life for one's friends."
—JOHN 15:13

After I came out, I found that most of my church friends, people I valued greatly and loved deeply, as if they were my very own brothers and sisters, mind you, no longer wanted anything to do with me. One by one, the message was loudly and clearly received as either calls went unanswered, I was told flat-out that so and so no longer wanted to speak to me, or as social media took hold, I was blocked online.

Everything about me for many of my former friends was now seen exclusively through the lens of homosexuality. Whispers that the way I probably blinked at them one time meant I must have been trying to lure them to the dark side as an act of satanic evil. It was both sad and highly comical. One day, I was just another guy. The next day, all my actions were seen through a prism of sex and sin.

One friend, whom I had such enormous love and respect for, whom I considered a brother, refused all communication. I was completely dumbfounded and hurt. His wife instead reached out eventually and said my friend no longer wished to speak to me. To add insult to injury, his younger sister, whom I had also known for years, just straight up meanly ignored me. Such Christian charity!

All of these people I had been close with were literally nowhere to be found anymore.

One former classmate wrote to me on Facebook several years after I had left the Christian school. He wanted to let me know via chat messenger that he had heard I was gay, and that while he did not condone my lifestyle, he had given it much prayer and thought and decided he could still be my friend.

I replied nicely that he completely misunderstood the assignment here. I was not in need of anyone deciding that they could be *my* friend. The question that needed an answer was did I want to be *his* or anyone else's friend. In this case, I chose not to be his friend. You see, I did not need someone feeling like they were doing me any favors, when the favor of my friendship was mine to give whenever and to whomever I graced with the awesomeness God granted me.

The thing that hurt my soul was that I really had loved these people like my own, like I was in fact commanded by Christ to do. But they, the ones I had the deepest spiritual relationships with, saw me as something unclean, that should not be touched or that one should not go near.

I struggled with this on two points. On the one hand, they must never have been my friends or brothers and sisters in Christ at all if it were conditional. It appeared that love was only love and friendship was only friendship if one met conditions or criteria.

On the other hand, if they really believed being gay was such a sin, why weren't they trying to envelop me in love? Why were they not reaching out even more than they had before to be there for me? Instead, unclean meant pariah, which also meant the most un-Christlike response one could give, and that was the one offered to me repeatedly and near universally. It was, "Do what I think you should do, be who I think you should be, or do not commune with me."

This was not true for everyone. A handful of my friends did not care one way or the other who I was attracted to—they just loved me for me.

There is a song that ponders, "What a friend we have in Jesus," and ain't it the truth? You see, Jesus and his Father, my Father, were my friends no matter who on this side of heaven wanted to be or not. Jesus gave his own skin to save mine. Now that's friendship!

I had to lean on these facts during those difficult times. Knowing that people fail us, that they are imperfect, but once again I AM never fails us at any moment of our lives. He was and is always my friend.

I was around eight or nine years old when I looked out the window of our home and saw that the house across the street was on fire. I screamed so loud, my father and one of my brothers came running up the stairs.

When my father saw the flames, he did not think twice before leaping into action. He ran out the front door and was across the street within seconds, as my mother got on the phone with the fire department.

After watching my father unsuccessfully try to open the front door of the neighbor's house, he threw his shoulder into it in an attempt to body slam it open. The door caved, but the rush of oxygen from the incoming air caused an explosion of fire and wind that threw my father's body off the stoop and onto the neighbor's front lawn.

Most people would have stopped there. In all honesty, most people would have stopped at calling the fire department. But with eyebrows singed off and lungs filled with smoke, my father was undeterred, and he marched around to the back door of the house.

He managed to get inside, and he recalls to this day how he was mere inches away from the male neighbor who was home, struggling to find his way out of the burning house. In the end, in a cloud of fire and smoke, their hands were unable to connect, and the neighbor disappeared into the flames and ultimately to his death.

That is the kind of friend I want. One who is willing to plunge into the fire repeatedly to save my life. I pray I am that kind of friend to others and that I would willingly lay down my life for theirs if the time came.

Fortunately, our ultimate friend has already done this for us all.

PRAYER

You are the most perfect friend, God. I count myself quadruple lucky in the friend department because I first have an infinite Father, you, the maker of all who is in all. I have my bestie Jesus, who gave everything for me and now keeps me whole through not only forgiveness but by being my intercessor and direct line to the eternal being, just as he is the eternal being at the same time.

I also have the Spirit that lives within my being and is able to speak for me when words cannot. Perfect friendship could not be any more complete, and for that I humbly and fully thank you!

I also thank you for those people in my life who are by my side through thick and thin, my earthly friends who are so important to my daily walk. Please bless these people and help me in turn to be a blessing and wonderful friend to them. Continue to bring people into my life whom I can form bonds with to edify each other and support each other, because these relationships help make me full and complete.

REFLECTION

1. What does friendship mean to me?
2. Which of my friendships are the deepest, and why?
3. How do I approach friendship with the eternal? Is it a strictly formal friendship, or do I communicate with God in informal ways as well, like I would any other friend?
4. How can I develop a more intimate friendship with God that threads throughout my days and nights and not just during times of need?

Homelessness

"Anyone who does not provide for their relatives, and especially for their own household, has denied the faith and is worse than an unbeliever."

—1 TIMOTHY 5:8

It might seem strange that in a book on Christian devotional topics, homelessness would be the subject of a chapter, but in the LGBTQ+ community, forced homelessness for our youth at the hands of religious parents is one of the most prevalent and pressing concerns.

According to the 2021 National Survey on LGBTQ+ Youth Mental Health, almost one third of all LGBTQ+ youth have been homeless at some point in their young lives. The main reason for LGBTQ+ homelessness is due to mistreatment at home by parents or caregivers due to sexual and/or gender identity.

The National Coalition for the Homeless cites that LGBTQ+ youth are 120 percent more likely to be homeless at some point than their non-LGBTQ+ counterparts.

These statistics are crushing, especially in light of many LGBTQ+ homeless youth sharing that acts and threats of physical and emotional violence at the hands of their parents or caregivers over religion are what ultimately lead to them either being kicked out of their homes or being forced to run away.

Think about that for a second.

Where in the Bible does Jesus say kick your kid's ass, or kick your kids out because of their sexuality or gender identity? What part of any of that even slightly aligns with Christ himself or his teachings?

I stood at the front door of our home when I was around six or seven, clutching onto my sister, as I watched my oldest brother bring boxes out one by one to his car.

My parents had converted in my youth, and we became disciplined members of an evangelical church that the rest of my family called "the cult."

The cult played a huge part in my life at many different stages. But at this moment, it had led to my parents kicking my gay teenage brother out of the house. Being gay was not an option in the cult and therefore in our home, regardless of what that meant in terms of my brother's living situation.

While the full story is his to tell, not mine, it serves to demonstrate that when one third of LGBTQ+ youth are forced out of their homes, you can guarantee that you know at least one gay, lesbian, or transgender person who has gotten the boot from the people who are supposed to love and protect them the most in this world.

At some point, my brother and parents must have reached a détente, because my brother moved back home. Yet not long after that, I was in the hall closet looking for a heating pad when the box that the heating pad was supposed to be in fell to the floor. From inside the box, several books spilled out. I picked them up and discovered a raft of manuals on how to convert your gay child to straight. My brother might have been back in our four walls, but the distaste for who he was as a person still existed. The books seemed to say, "You might live here, but who you are is not welcome."

Later on, in my own teenage years, I also attempted to come out to my mother. At the time, she insisted emphatically on all that lived and breathed that it was not so. She kept saying that God had told her I would get married and have children. While she was speaking to me, I heard my father at the bottom of the stairs creep away. He had apparently been listening.

I am certain it is only because my brother had broken down the wall a few years back that I didn't suffer the same fate he had and wasn't myself moving boxes of my clothes into my car to take to the streets.

In later years, my mother apologized numerous times for the way she treated my brother and then to a far lesser degree me in terms of our sexuality. My mother, being especially religious, came to the studied conclusion as she grew that in the scheme of all things, one's sexuality, and frankly gender, did not matter. I say gender as well because when she found out I did drag, she laughed and said she thought that was great fun. She then rattled off a list of drag personas from television and film that she and my father enjoyed, specifically landing, to my surprise, on the character of Madea played by Tyler Perry. She asked me if I thought I was transgender and said that if I was, she would still love me.

One day, only a few years ago, she turned to me and said, "If you had to be gay, I am so glad you are with the person you are with." She went on to say how she knew emphatically that God had placed my partner in my life and that while she was so insistent when I was younger that I could not be gay because God said to her I would be married, she realized now that God's marriage plans for me were my husband. She continued and told me that she had, like most humans do, such limited sight back when she was younger and that she was trying to force God and his plans into her ideas of love and marriage, not realizing until she had matured that God's plans are not always clear through our limited vision until we are at the point where can truly see and understand those plans. In the end, she shared how she would have done many things differently when it came to my brother and me. She would have embraced, and perhaps even celebrated who we are.

Parents are meant to be the ultimate caregivers. Yes, there is most certainly a role for shaping, disciplining, and working to lay out the best path one can for one's children. In the end, though, love and acceptance must be unconditional, the way God's love for us is unconditional.

It is not "tough love" to kick a child out onto the sidewalk, a common phrase you hear when someone wants to justify their actions. This is especially true over something as basic as sexuality or gender. Trust me when I say that so many LGBTQ+ youth at some point in their lives would tell you they would be glad to give up a limb to not have been born the way they are so that they wouldn't have to deal with all the bullshit and hatred people throw their way. I know firsthand because I felt this same way numerous times in my life! Who would choose to be an outcast that is constantly ridiculed or worse? No one.

Parents should hold their children near when they feel safe enough to reveal their true selves. After all, if you don't love your child once you learn they are gay or that their body doesn't reflect who they are on the inside, then frankly you never really loved them at all. In most cases, though, parents really know all along who their children are, so the feigned shock and righteous indignation is just an opportunity to throw a tantrum about their worries over how others will view them and their parenting. Often, little of it has to do with their care or feelings for their child.

Let me make it perfectly clear—people do not choose their sexual orientation. Neither do people arbitrarily choose their gender. We are born who we are born.

There is a grave misconception among the religious that these things are limited to X or Y and that anything outside of the X and Y in their minds is not natural. Yet, when we look at the animal kingdom, we find lifelong gay partners in penguins who raise babies together; we find homosexual acts among all kinds of creatures that walk, crawl, fly, and swim; we find fish and insects that are born one sex and then morph into another sex at different points of their lives; we find beings that impregnate themselves without the help of a male or female partner; we even find humans born with both sex organs.

Sex and gender are a mish-mash rainbow across all of Earth's inhabitants.

It is a complete waste of energy arguing over such garbage or trying to change something innate in another being. Our time should instead be focused on loving others, spreading joy, and welcoming people into our homes, not kicking them out.

There are LGBTQ+ people both young and old in the United States and around the world who have no roof over their heads because of the way God in heaven created them. If God created these beautiful people, who is anyone else to stand against them?

PRAYER

God, I am thankful when I have a safe space to live, a roof over my head where my physical, emotional, and spiritual being is not in any danger. Help me, Father, to pray for, think of, and give back to others elsewhere in this world who do not have this safe space. Just as I am safe, may all LGBTQ+ people find comfort and peace in a loving home of their own, no matter what part of the world they live in.

REFLECTION

1. Am I aware of the plight of LGBTQ+ youth in our country and the world? Was I aware prior to reading this chapter on the pressing homelessness situation that confronts so many?

69

2. What experiences do I have with homelessness, whether directly or that of others?

3. In what ways might these challenges that our youth face affect their views on God? How can I be a light sharing his light in their darkest hours and in the years afterward?

4. How can I have an impact on this issue both here and abroad?

5. What organizations exist that face the LGBTQ+ homelessness issue head-on, and are there ways I can support these organizations?

Fear

"When I am afraid, I put my trust in you. In God, whose word I praise—
in God I trust and am not afraid. What can mere mortals do to me?"

—PSALMS 56:3–4

Everyone knows fear in their lives. There are fears, however, that gays, lesbians, transgender and nonconforming individuals experience that are unique from the regular fears others face. Often, the perception of how one presents themselves in different aspects of their lives can have all kinds of consequences that do not exist for cisgender or heterosexual men and women.

Concern over physical safety is ever present in the minds of our community. If we walk, talk, or move the wrong way, it can mean the end of our lives. For untold thousands of transgender people, just presenting as their true selves ultimately led to their deaths. There are an almost unbelievable number of assaults and murders of trans and non-gender-conforming people in the United States every year. Many of these go unreported out of grave fear that they will be further abused by law enforcement—that is, if they were fortunate enough to even have survived at the hands of their perpetrators of violence.

Recently, in New York City, a young man was killed at a gas station for voguing, a popular style of dance associated with the gay ballroom scene. Someone got so heated over the fact that this kid was dancing in a "gay" manner while his friends pumped gas that they stabbed him. Several years before this incident, one trans woman was walking down the street in the Bronx and got hit from behind with a two by four, instantly killing her. She never even saw it coming.

I have known many people, unfortunately, who have been hit, kicked, and body slammed, had their hair pulled, and had their bodies violently violated for no reason other than that someone thought it was not only acceptable but admirable to attack homosexuals and transgender people. Outside of the fear of physical violence, there are other fears that exist for LGBTQ+ people.

These include the ever-present danger of verbal harassment. I for one have been called every name in the book while daring to walk past strangers, whether I was dressed as a boy or a girl. For many years, I used to do my best to make myself as small as possible out of fear of being verbally attacked and called names. It actually took me years post high school to get to a point where I didn't automatically think people were talking about me if I heard a group of strangers laughing.

On top of abuse, LGBTQ+ folks have limited job opportunities in comparison to our peers. We know we don't just have to dance backward in heels, but we also have to recite the preamble to the Constitution while we blink twice on every third beat of the music in order to even be considered for a promotion.

I have never before shared the following story outside of with my partner.

Several years back, I was up for a position advancement at a regular day job. Truth be told, I ran circles around the other candidates in terms of the quality and quantity of their work. My productivity was such that my bosses repeatedly assigned me the toughest tasks and told me constantly that the reason I was assigned this work was because I was the best at the job. They also referred others on the team to me for ways to improve their work. On top of that, they would parade me out to lead large group training sessions for the field, as they felt I excelled at leading professional development.

About a week after I had applied for the position, two colleagues announced at a team meeting that they had each been promoted to the new managerial roles. The supervisors publicly lauded them and announced that these selections were approved. In other words, that was all she wrote. There were no other open positions. I was completely shocked—I hadn't even been interviewed yet.

I asked to meet with one of my supervisors, and she agreed to do so. We went into her office, and I asked her why I hadn't been interviewed and how the positions could have been filled already without this taking place, since there was a strict hiring and promotion protocol.

She looked me straight in the eye and said, "We decided you were not presentable enough for a leadership position."

The air deflated from both my lungs and my spirit. I asked what she meant by not presentable.

We both knew exactly what she meant.

Here I was in ultraliberal New York City, where gays are a dime a dozen, and I was openly being denied a job because they did not want a gay man to represent their office.

It was fine to wheel me out in front of large groups, as effeminate gay humor is hilarious from a safe distance. Especially when they could put me back in my clown car at the end. It was equally okay to assign me the most difficult tasks, because I made them look good when I was successful.

It was not, however, acceptable to have me be a face for the office because, well that was uncomfortable. What might others think when I walked in the room? What message would they be conveying if a gay man were representing them?

One of my greatest fears had come true. Someone had humiliated me by letting my sexuality and my mannerisms negatively influence their decisions on my worth as a person.

I went home that day dejected. Should I stay at a job that had just stomped me into the ground? Fear of keeping a roof over my head and food on my table were real.

Did I sue them for violating my rights? The thought of putting my energy into a nasty lawsuit that could not only take years, but where I would have to share my humiliation publicly, weighed on my heart.

I was afraid to even search for a new job, as there had to be something about me that they saw that was so flamingly gross that they, and anyone else, couldn't possibly work with. It took me back to the reason I had changed my major in college away from Biblical Studies. I was back to the question: Who would want to work with me as a gay man? What worth did I have?

Soon afterward, though, I could hear the power of God's word coming through my spirit. "For I am the Lord your God who takes hold of your right hand and says to you, Do not fear; I will help you." (Isaiah 41:13).

With those words on my heart and mind, I silently simmered for a hot minute before I decided to find a new job. I ultimately reached out to someone and secured a new position. Why the supervisor who told me I was not presentable acted completely surprised that I left, I still do not understand. Maybe it was to cover their own ass in case I sued.

While I was the one to pull the plug on that job, the potential for job loss if one is discovered to be gay or lesbian, or if one comes to work dressed as one's true gender identity, weighs heavy, even in these days where it seems pride flies high around our country.

We have not even touched on the constant fear of losing family and friends when one comes out of the closet or begins to live fully as who they truly are.

Prior to writing this book, I took more than a hot minute to decide whether or not I was in the mental position to handle the tempest that might follow its publishing. After all, I have written for numerous publications over the course of my drag life, and one thing has been constant.

Whenever you put yourself out there in print, people come out with their knives to slice and dice you if they disagree, even if they never read another word you wrote beyond the title.

As I prepared for this Christian book as a drag queen author, I recognized instantly that in the times we live in, where mass shootings, physical brutality, political uprisings, and the constant tearing down that happens on social media are the norm, I was taking a risk. My fleshly being could be in danger. My day-to-day life could be affected. My psyche could be attacked by an onslaught of haters. This might sound dramatic on some level if you've never experienced the homo-bashing nature of our world, but that unfortunately is the reality that exists when you are gay, when you do drag and dress in women's clothing, and when you become a mouthpiece for important causes.

I once jokingly referred to the actress Susan Sarandon as Susan Saranwrap in an article on the 2016 election, riffing on how her support for one candidate might have cost another candidate an election win. Someone responded that everyone in New York City hated me and that I was going to die. In this case, I would not just be writing about an election or even LGBTQ+ issues at large, but instead I would be joining the call for a reexamining of our religious values and texts. Our systems of religion have enshrined exclusion into their bedrock principles for so long that pushback and outright anger would be unavoidable.

Then, the verse at the start of this chapter came to my mind. There are so many other wonderful pieces of scripture that speak to the power of God and his ability to overcome all of our fears.

This one resonated particularly, though, for where I was at in facing my own fears of writing this book. I was to put my trust in God and to stand on his word. After all, there is absolutely nothing out there that God himself cannot conquer. What could mere mortals do to me? They could gnash their teeth. They could roar their heads off. But they could not conquer God or his word.

To my LGBTQ+ brothers and sisters, and equally for our beautiful and important allies, there is nothing that can stand against us with God on our side. Paul hit the nail on the head in Romans chapter 8 when he said, "For I am convinced that neither death nor life, neither angels nor demons, neither the present nor the future, nor any powers, neither height nor depth, nor anything else in all creation, will be able to separate us from the love of God that is in Christ Jesus our Lord."

Freaking angels and demons cannot even get in between what God and I got? Fear just kinda melts away when you realize not even a Marvel Universe villain could stand against God.

Seek out God, and in doing so you will have everything you need to stare down and defeat fear. When my knees buckle in life, the first place I go is to his throne. He lifts from me any fears I have, no matter what they are, and he can do the same for you.

"I lift up my eyes to the hills. From where does my help come? My help comes from the Lord, who made heaven and earth." (Psalms 121:1–2 ESV)

PRAYER

You are so powerful, Father in heaven, that all fear melts away when you are near. The infinite master who could zap this planet into oblivion in the blink of an eye, the way you created this world and all that is in it in the same manner. With your strength, help me to release all fears, Lord, and to give them fully over to you. You can handle the things I cannot. Jesus says he will take our burdens, and I freely hand those over to you, and feel the weight of fear lift from my shoulders and spirit. With you for me, who in this world or beyond is powerful enough to stand against me? None, and so with that reassuring knowledge, fear has no power over me because Jesus lives and I AM reigns supreme.

REFLECTION

1. What am I most fearful of?

2. What are my go-to responses when faced with frightening situations?

3. In what ways has fear kept me from stepping out and doing the things I want to do or being the person I want to be?

4. How can my relationship with God improve my ability to step out and face down those fears?

God's Timing

"The Lord is good to those whose hope is in him, to the one who seeks him; it is good to wait quietly for the salvation of the Lord."

—LAMENTATIONS 3:25–26

Patience is the one virtue I missed when being created in heaven's baby factory. The patience conveyor belt either had a technical snafu, or the angel in charge took a bathroom break when my little personhood rolled on by.

Like most people, I suspect, I want everything done yesterday/last week. What I have come to find out in my passage of faith is that things do not work on my time, but God's. I found this to be especially maddening and incredibly awe-inspiring when it came to my student loans.

This journey is one I know will make some scratch their heads and others recognize the way God methodically and ever so skillfully works in our lives when he knows our beginnings and our endings. It does not speak to the immediacy of resolution but speaks to my own limited sight that failed to see or understand how a tiny particle blown on the wind by God's breath can over many years lead to the most perfectly timed hurricane.

Following the completion of my master's degree, I found myself drowning in student loan debt. I often wonder why on earth we give children the power to take out tens of thousands of dollars in college aid when they do not yet know there ass from their elbows, much less who they even are in life?

Alas, I was in my early twenties and saddled with an insurmountable bill after attending a private university. To be frank, I didn't know or understand a damn thing when I signed my life away to the slavery of student debt at such a young and completely oblivious age. Yet here I was.

One of the only ways I could manage the debt was to go back to school yet again, because the job I had landed would not cover the minimum payment for the loans. With no choice then, I attended some additional schooling. Not because I wanted to by any stretch of the imagination. It was because I had to, since deferment was automatic if I was enrolled in school. However, that just led to a terrible cycle I could not get out of, because more schooling equaled both deferment and a higher debt load. It was like a tiny speck of sand that first started to roll down from the top of a mountain when I first entered college and eventually turned into an unstoppable avalanche that I could not get away from.

Eventually, I landed a moderately decent-paying job, at least on paper, in New York City. I say on paper because one's salary in New York City can look decent or even great if one lived anyplace else, but with the price of survival often doubled or tripled, the taxable income might sound high while the take-home pay and the power of the dollar are pitifully low.

Side note—most drag queens have full-time jobs, as it costs a lot of damn money to do drag. Almost 100 percent of drag performers are not able to make a living on drag alone. In fact, in my case, almost anything I ever made doing drag I either put right back into buying clothes, wigs, makeup, etc. or I donated directly to charity. To sum it up, nine-to-five she's a plain ole working girl. Five-to-nine she's too fabulous for words.

Now, mind you, every step along the way I would reach out to the holders of my student loans and ask for them to work with me on a feasible payment plan, because otherwise I had no choice but to become homeless. They repeatedly told me that under no circumstances would they work with me. I had to pay the number they asked for each month or go into default. Let me repeat that—the student loan companies told me I should default instead of making a smaller payment because they would not work with me on any level, and I mean literally any level, to lower my payments even temporarily.

Repeatedly over the years, I found myself begging and pleading with God to intervene. At times, I felt myself stuck between a choice to either not pay the loans yet remain living in my apartment and buying food, or to pay them but live on the streets of NYC. I didn't own a car, so I would have had to show up to work each day in the same clothes, unshowered, since New York subway tunnels do not have shower facilities for those living in cardboard boxes. I prayed, but no answer came. At least, I did not think so.

I exhausted every deferment and forbearance allowed to me over the course of years. I spent honestly untold days and hours crying on my knees, falling to the floor to beg over and over for help.

Dealing with the stress of my student loans was the one and only time in my life where I questioned my faith. Why was God not helping me? He was my whole life, and I knew that with a half blink of his left eye he could wipe away all student debt, including mine. With one tiny thought, he could force the loan company to feel compassion and reduce my payment to something affordable.

The student loan system in the United States is set up to be a form of modern slavery. It is a racket in its simplest form. Young and naive teenagers sign away their lives to predatory lenders for tens of thousands of dollars from which there is no escape. Teens do not know enough about life or finances to understand what they are getting themselves into. Unlike other forms of debt, where millionaires and billionaires can declare bankruptcy yet walk away keeping their mansions, furs, private jets, and jewels, student loan borrowers have no escape. They are chained to their youthful debts of ignorance for their entire lives. There is no escape clause, no bankruptcy option.

To further compound the problem, the student loan companies profit exponentially more if the owner of the debt defers or even heaven forbid defaults. Interest on student loans was designed to legally balloon, thereby making my original debt of $80,000 swell to $486,000 over the course of my years since college. You are reading that correctly—I could not fully pay the 80K I owed immediately on my salary in New York City, so instead they quickly blew it up through minimum payments, forbearance, and deferments that I was forced into taking until my total reached almost half a million dollars instead.

My story felt like that of Job. Job was a wealthy and God-fearing man, so much so that God and Satan had a little bet that if God took everything away from Job, he would remain faithful. As his life collapsed around him, Job lashed out at God because he believed that God had left him.

I'm somewhat embarrassed to admit that I felt so broken and so forsaken that I even contemplated suicide. I felt like I could never get out of this embarrassingly impossible cycle that would keep me down for, and destroy, the rest of my life. There was no way out whatsoever . . . or so I thought.

When I was at my lowest, I continued praying and pleading and asking God, like Job did, why he had forsaken me. I kept receiving in my prayers the same message back: "Oh ye of little faith."

When Christ and his apostles were on a boat in the sea, a giant storm came up. Jesus was asleep, so his disciples woke him with great fear. He chastised them with the same words above, then calmed the seas.

I also heard, "With the Lord a day is like a thousand years and a thousand years is like a day." (2 Peter 3:8). These verses and many others swirled through my head throughout the years of my student loan struggles. God was clearly telling me to sit back and watch his power that would play out on his time right before my weak-faith eyes.

Throughout this whole time, I still spent many nights sleepless and in tears with worry over how I would ever pay back half a million dollars.

I was down to my last teardrop, as I was set to begin increasing monthly payments with funds that I did not have the power to generate, when an unexpected letter came in the mail.

The letter thanked me for my many years of service in the public arena and informed me that based on my years at my day job, and my meeting of the qualified number of payments over the course of these many years, my loans were completely forgiven.

I physically fell to the floor. I spread myself out with my face on the ground and thanked God and the love of Jesus over and over for seeing me through this never-ending nightmare. What came to me were the very words I'd heard the first time I cried and asked if I was being forsaken.

God had always had a plan. I was just too small, as was my faith to fully see or understand it. He had already started the first lever moving years and years back, but I was too blind to recognize it. My limited sight was unable to grasp the pieces of the puzzle that were one by one falling into place over time, his time.

I did not get instant relief back in the day when I was first challenged with repayment. Instead, I received the gift of seeing God move a mountain on my behalf over my lifetime so that in my maturity, I would recognize and acknowledge his greatness and love for me.

I share this deeply personal and, prior to today, highly private story with you for several important reasons. I would have taken my financial struggles over student debt to the grave but for the fact that like the blind man Jesus healed who ran out and told everyone, I cannot help but share how God released me here in this book of faith and devotion. I already had victory and freedom in Christ Jesus, but God rescued me from the trials of this temporal life as well, and I have an obligation and a joyful reason to share it.

Second, God is infinite. Our lives are but a blip in time. For anyone impatient like me, lessons can be long and feel painful, but he knows better than us when and in what manner respite should and will come.

Third, we are all weak. We all have moments of doubt. We all have those low times when we feel like we can't go on because the path ahead of us seems impossible. Yet it is in these times especially that we need to let go of our instinct to control things. We must trust that God has a plan that we do not presently have the capability to understand, then hold on to that faith and keep stepping forward in our lives. The answers we are looking for, or the ones the Lord has for us that we do not even know about yet, are likely better for us, could already be in action. A pebble hits the water, but the ripples ring out farther and farther across the surface over time, not in the first moment of impact.

In the end, "Job replied to the LORD 'I know that you can do all things; no purpose of yours can be thwarted. You asked, "Who is this that obscures my plans without knowledge?" Surely I spoke of things I did not understand, things too wonderful for me to know. You said, "Listen now, and I will speak; I will question you, and you shall answer me." My ears had heard of you but now my eyes have seen you. Therefore I despise myself and repent in dust and ashes.'" (Job 42)

Though our humanity cries out for instant results, let us step back and let the power of God unfold in his time, not ours.

PRAYER

Things unfold in your time, Lord, not mine. Help me to overcome my shortsightedness and know that you alone can see the bigger picture. You know what is right for me and have the right timeline to meet my needs. May I learn to trust in you patiently and fully.

REFLECTION

1. What are the things in my life that I can give over to God knowing that I may not have the resolution I am seeking for a short or long period

of time to come? Can I accept that he knows best and will handle all of these things in his way and in his time?

2. At which points in my life have I seen God's plans come to fruition? Were any of the results surprising, and if so, where do I see God's hand in these results?

Illness

"The Lord will strengthen him on his bed of illness;
You will sustain him on his sickbed."

—PSALMS 41:3 (NKJV)

When I graduated high school, I first attended one of New York State's universities. Toward the end of my sophomore year, I felt like I pulled a muscle in my right shoulder. I was at home visiting my parents for spring break and mentioned it to my mother. She made the point that as long as I was home for a week or so, I might as well have the doctor look at it since I kept complaining about the pain.

The doctor decided it would be best to get a quick x-ray of my shoulder in case I tore something or there was a sprain or break somewhere. The image was taken, and it showed nothing wrong with my shoulder at all. In fact, from the moment the x-ray machine clicked, I never once had another pain in my shoulder again. It was gone. However, the doctor ushered us into his office to tell us that the left side of the x-ray happened to catch something unrelated—what appeared to be an enlarged heart. He recommended that we go see a cardiologist, as it was likely that I had pericarditis, which is essentially a cold or infection in the heart. This would probably lead to my needing to take a round of antibiotics.

That didn't seem too traumatic, so off we trotted to one of Long Island's top cardiologists, who was a family acquaintance and therefore had agreed to see us ASAP, as I was set to return to college within days. My mother and I sat in the waiting room, discussing where we would go out to lunch after the appointment. They called me into the examination room, and numerous tests later, we were sitting in comfortable chairs in the doctor's well-appointed office. I looked out past him onto the beautifully sunny day, barely paying any attention to what he was saying, figuring my mother would get the skinny and pick up whatever pills I needed. Suddenly, my mother started to cry, so I directed my attention back to the conversation that I had tuned out of.

"Wait. What?" I heard myself say, as their conversation centered around the hole in my heart and my urgent need for open heart surgery.

Apparently, I had been walking around since birth with an open space in my heart that a flap of skin was supposed to naturally cover over the moment I took my first breath. As a result, I had been weaker and more prone to illness throughout my youth, but none of us had given it too much thought. Yeah I got the flu and colds a bunch, but many kids do.

The reason for the sudden urgency was that one side of my heart was pumping twice as much blood as the other side and had blown up exponentially. Without surgery, my heart was likely to give out in the near future.

Talk about whiplash! I had gone to one doctor for a shoulder pain that never existed and wound up at a different doctor in need of emergency surgery to save my life when I hadn't even known it was in danger mere hours earlier.

All the praise goes to God, because that shoulder pain had to have been heaven-sent. The surgery was successful as you can tell, since I'm old as Methuselah and still around to annoy the crap out of everyone.

More recently, I came home one day to find my partner bundled up in bed with a fever of over 104 degrees. He was completely burning up and drenched with sweat. Earlier that day, he'd been fine, but now he had terrible back pain and couldn't move, on top of the high temperature. I had never seen him sick like this and with that temperature, so the emergency room seemed like the only logical solution.

As soon as we stepped inside the hospital, my partner was on a gurney, and a gaggle of seven or eight doctors circled him while they rolled him away, peppering him with questions and taking his vitals. They seemed to be incredibly concerned about his state of health, and I watched helplessly as he was carted down the hall.

Once the initial review was over, groups of doctors would periodically come by to ask him or me the same questions over and over. However, he was not getting the relief from the symptoms he was exhibiting. They demonstrated grave concern for whatever was happening with him but had no answers as to the cause. Antibiotics and acetaminophen had failed to bring down the fever, and blood tests weren't indicating anything easily identifiable. So there he sat, hour after hour.

Something I have learned all too well over the past few years is that unless you have someone to advocate for you in hospitals, you are less likely to get the appropriate medical attention you need. Not that hospital staff are purposefully inattentive or anything. It's that they are so often completely overwhelmed that it can be unavoidable to not give everyone the attention they need despite their best efforts. A gnat in the ear can be an effective help, and being a royal pain in the ass is something I confess I am somewhat of an expert in.

Things came to a head when I dragged a nurse over to give my partner something, anything to relieve his excruciating back pain. When she offered him one of those over-the-counter back pain relief patches, he lost his mind. He started pulling all of the hospital garb off, yelling that he could go to the pharmacy for that and didn't need to be sitting there in the hospital for hours in pain for a cheap medicated patch.

I ran off and brought a doctor with me this time, who let us know that while they couldn't figure out yet what exactly was wrong, if he left the hospital there was a risk of death, potentially from sepsis. I talked my partner into staying under, and they administered some strong pain medication and decided he would need to be admitted.

As he sat in the bed shivering, half in and out, I prayed fervently. The story of Hezekiah from 2 Kings 20 swam into my mind.

Hezekiah was a king of Judah. God sent Isaiah to Hezekiah to tell him to put his affairs in order, as he was about to die. Hezekiah did not want to die, so he pleaded with God to let him live, and as a result, God granted Hezekiah fifteen more years of life.

I prayed that God would grant my partner more years to his life if it was his will.

With nothing left to do but sit there in the hospital for hours, I composed a song as a means of prayer.

Make me a Hezekiah, Lord
I pray add fifteen to my life
Move the shadow back ten steps
Before I go to paradise
This body is weak, but this spirit is not
And I'll yet do good in your eyes
Make me a Hezekiah, Lord
I'm just not ready to die

To be clear, I am not foolishly suggesting that every time we want someone to get better all we have to do is pray and voilà, they will be healed. I am saying that God has the ability to heal. All things are by his will. When everything was said and done in this case, my partner survived.

In Philippians, it says that in every situation, you are to present your requests to God. We are supposed to ask. We may not always get the answer we want, because we don't have the discernment of the eternal who sees things beyond our understanding, but we can and should ask.

PRAYER

I pray to you, Father, through Jesus your Son, for healing in my life and the lives of others. May those who I name be made whole through your great power. Help me to accept your will, dear God, as I am too small to understand your master plan. I know the natural world you created leads some to suffer natural causes, but I also know you are there with us to see us through to healing or heaven. I give to you all of the physical, psychological, emotional, and spiritual ailments of myself and those I love. I hand these over to you knowing you are the all-knowing, all-powerful, all-wise God.

REFLECTION

1. Who in my life is in need of healing, either physically or emotionally?

2. What is my role in the healing of others and myself?

3. What do I believe is God's role in healing?

4. Where do I need help accepting outcomes that are too painful to bear?

Strength

Over the last several years, members of my family have been plagued with critical medical issues that left me in the position to make decisions regarding their healthcare. It is no easy task to be the one whose words carry the weight of life-altering implications for anyone other than yourself.

One of these decisions happened three years ago. I was at the beach on the New Jersey Shore with my partner, having a gay ole time, when my cell phone began to blow up. I listened to the first voicemail that came through, and it was my father telling me something was seriously wrong with my mother and that she was acting funny.

The voicemail said she'd started saying things that made no sense whatsoever, so my father brought her to her doctor, who felt that my mother, who has a history of strange stomach problems, had potentially overdosed on stomach proton-inhibitors. Many people take these over- the-counter antacids that help with things like Reflux and GERD. He felt, based on the conversation with my mom, that she had gone hog wild that day and taken a handful. To be safe, they sent her to the ER, where the doctor's conclusion was confirmed and she was sent home.

This was when the phone calls to me on the beach began, post the hospital visit. I was not too alarmed, as per the voicemail, the hospital had just seen her, so I calmly called back to get the low-down, and speak to her directly.

My first interaction with her told me immediately this was not an Omeprezole overdose, and that I needed to be more worried than the hospital appeared to be. She was not making any sense with what she was saying and kept referring to me as my oldest brother, insisting that I was him no matter how many times I told her whom she was speaking with. She also began slurring her words. This led to my insistence for a rushed trip to a different emergency room.

Within hours, the second hospital found a tumor in her brain that was causing a large amount of swelling throughout the frontal lobe. This swelling was in turn messing up chunks of the brain beyond the tumor's location, impacting her thoughts, speech, and body movements. They brought in a brain surgeon who made it clear that there was no choice but to remove the tumor.

My mother has always been a battleax, to say the least. She is notoriously both smart as a whip and tough as nails. When you combine that with her being one of those "it-factor" people who can walk into a room and steal the spotlight, and charm the spots off a leopard, or at least talk them into believing they are in fact a giraffe, the hospital staff were no match. With half her brain swollen, she still managed to convince the learned expert doctors and the brain surgeon that she should go home for a few days to prepare for the surgery rather than do it right away. In retrospect, that was not the best decision, as all of that continued swelling for two additional days ultimately became the cause of a very difficult recovery and a more limited bounce back than if she had gone into the operating room immediately. But she convinced them all and she got her way, and as a result, she was sitting at home when I arrived after a frantic six-hour drive to get there.

When I did arrive at my parent's house, my mother began peppering me with questions about her diagnosis. I had spoken to the doctor during my car journey, so she needed me to tell her everything I had learned. At this point, most people whose brains were swollen would have been post-surgery or far more compliant given the situation. Not my mother. Everything in her was still about how she could control the situation.

Beyond the medical implications, she began hammering me with all of the information I needed to know regarding my sister, who at the nearly the same age as me, was of limited ability, having been diagnosed several years prior with white matter brain disease. Thus, my mother took care of all of my sister's needs, particularly financial, as my sister received disability. Though my sister had some moderate independence, she lived on my parents' farm property, just in another house very close by, so my parents could keep daily track of what she was doing.

For two days, my mother dragged me through file after file, making lists of what to do for my sister, how to pay her bills, etc. She also questioned me over and over again about what was wrong with her brain and why she needed to have the tumor removed.

Mind you, she would be half with it in one breath and sound lucid, like herself, and in the next be saying wildly unconnected things and calling me by different names, including the dog's.

At last, the night before the surgery, before I walked out the door to go sleep at my sister's house, my mother handed me a note. I want to share that I'm the youngest of my parents' birth children, though they did adopt in their elder years. My mother and I have a very deep connection, and she, like I said before, with literally half a brain functioning, was still a smart cookie. She knew clearly that I am the most emotional and sensitive of all of her children. It is not even a debated question, I just am. So she strategically handed me this note that I read as I walked up to my sister's house.

The letter emphatically implored me to stop her surgery from happening the next day. She wrote in this letter how I was the only person on this planet who could stop the removal of the tumor from taking place and that she was depending on me to do this for her. She made clear that she was aware that she would never fully recover once this surgery took place and that she would in many ways cease being herself in the way we all knew her.

OMG! I could not handle this level of Jewish guilt on top of everything else. (We might have converted religiously, but culturally we remain very much Jewish!)

The doctor felt there was a strong case that over time after surgery, she would bounce fully back, but with brains being tricky and her age as a factor—she was seventy-eight at the time—there were no guarantees. My mother however, had somehow surmised that the woman she was at present and had been her whole life would cease to exist once she went under the knife.

To a large degree, she wound up being correct, but did that even matter? Without the surgery, she was set to at best lose her ability to walk and slowly fade away from existence. At worst, and more likely, she would die.

Here I was, holding this note scribbled in barely legible script, with a terrible decision resting in my hands.

Should I step in and stop the surgery? Without it, she was going to die soon. Should I let the surgery take place even though she was clear she would never be the same?

I did not doubt her inner sight, despite the brain swelling. Sometimes, people know themselves better than all the doctors and tests combined.

I did not have the strength to make this decision, so I crumpled into a pile of hysterical tears in my sister's spare bedroom.

Ultimately, since I was the one who took the lead for everything with my mother's health at this time, as my father was also seventy-eight and had never in his life had to deal with any of the things my mother handled daily, it felt like everything was on my shoulders.

All I could do was pray. I knew God would guide me. So I blew up the phone to my brothers first, and then the phone to heaven next, for hours and hours until the next morning arrived.

As dawn broke, I walked outside and sat in front of my sister's house, looking out on peaceful fields filled with bales of hay my father had recently gathered. To the side of the one large field that I was looking upon at that moment was a forest.

As I glanced at the trees, I prayed aloud. I know the Bible says we should not put the Lord to the test. But I was too weak to deal with everything that was laid out in front of me at the moment. I just needed some help with my decisions for this day. I needed strength to see all of this through.

My mother has such a close relationship with God, and since I do too, I talked to him about that relationship between them and about how I knew that whatever his will was, whether she was to live or die, it was right for my mother.

I knew then that the surgery must go forward, and had peace in my heart.

I did cry a little more, because the human in me was full of fear, doubtful that I had the strength to get through what was about to happen. So, I said to God that it would be so comforting if I could have a sign that everything was going to be okay. That he was going to be with me no matter what happened. I chuckled aloud that something like a deer coming out of the woods right where my eyes were looking at that moment would be wonderful.

What happened next terrified me at first, then brought an inexplicable wave of strength, resolve, and calmness.

Right in the spot where my eyes were cast upon the woods, suddenly, a doe hopped out.

I gasped. The deer trotted out across the field. It reached midway, where it stopped and looked in my direction. Tears streamed down my face.

Out of the corner of my eye, a little twitch took place, so I turned back to where the deer had emerged from the woods only to see a second leap right out and joyfully bound its way over to the first.

I was amazed. It seemed like God was giving me an emphatic "I got you!"

When the second deer stopped by the first, once again, a twinkle of brown fur stirred within the same woods, at the exact same spot I had asked God to send out the first one as a sign, and yet a third deer walked out.

I sat there in an equal mix of both stupefied amazement and complete understanding that my answer was clear. My mother needed this surgery, and all was going to be just fine, no matter how difficult it seemed now. I had the strength to handle whatever was to come my way.

Some will read my words and think I must believe every time we ask God for a sign, he is going to dole it out and astound us. However, the Bible states clearly that God and Jesus have already performed numerous signs, and so many miracles. In fact, the demonstrations have been laid out so plentifully that at this point, if people still do not believe, that is really their issue. Jesus rose from the dead, for goodness' sake, and if that is not enough for one to embrace Christianity, nothing ever will be.

Yet, I do believe that in spite of the natural world God created, where he lets things play out, there are times when you knock and ask, and the door opens and miracles and signs still take place.

I asked for a deer, and I got three. I was filled with strength to handle the weeks and months ahead, which were difficult to say the least. But my mother went off to surgery and thankfully is still alive to this day.

Signs or no signs, God gives us the strength to do what needs to be done. To make choices, to stand firm.

Philippians 4:13 reads, "I can do all things through Christ who strengthens me." (NKJV)

We are so incredibly empowered as Christians. To begin with, we are not alone. We have the creator, we have the intercessor, and we have the spirit who guides us. We are really quite unstoppable!

Most often, our strength is something others do not ever get to see. We are in situations where we need to either gird our loins for an onslaught or make tough choices, and this type of strength that is required is inner, but no less important that the outer physical strength required in other situations.

At first, doing drag took a lot of inner strength and was the result of a lot of prayer.

This will likely shock those wackadoodles who are on what they believe to be a God-inspired crusade to rid the nation and world of drag entertainers, but God was very much at the forefront of my drag activity.

I always had an interest in the arts, but I was far too scared to ever put myself out there with anything that involved performance. For many years, I said to myself and others that one day, I was going to produce something for film or television, but the years ticked by and I never found the time or bravery to do anything but talk about it. Until one day, when out of nowhere, I became inspired to write a web series about drag queen superheroes.

My inspiration was an antigay demonstration I had seen on TV news where a bunch of men and women held signs about how gays were going to hell while attending a funeral of a gay man.

In my mind, I could not think of anything less like Jesus than these protestors. It made me reflect on how foolish these people were. For all they knew, God might have been incredibly involved in the life of the man whose funeral they picketed.

God has a long habit of using people the world finds worthless to spread his message and demonstrate his power. Jesus himself had a prostitute, an adulteress, a murder, and more in his genealogy. Moses was a terrible mouthpiece for God, so much so that his brother Aaron had to do his speaking, yet he was one of the most influential Jews who ever lived. I could go on and on about Jesus dining with sinners, God's prophets being messes, and so on, but the point rests on the fact that it is often not the perfect or pious that God has been shown to work through, but those who would be otherwise tossed aside.

In a time where gays, lesbians, etc. are attacked, perhaps art could illustrate that the ones we deem weakest are the possessors of strength at its greatest. Hence drag queens, who mainstream America, and certainly what I term evangelicals who thought they were doing God's bidding, considered absolute deviant trash, would be the perfect vehicle for demonstrating strength and goodness.

Further, Jezebel from the bible was so universally considered wicked that to this day her name is used to splash a giant evil whore symbol across a person. So I rolled all that up into a great big rainbow ball, and out poured "Jeza and the Belles," a web series about three drag sisters who save the world from destruction.

I had a public-facing job at the time, so while I launched into self-producing the web series, I was worried about how if anyone found out about my writing and producing something about drag queens, I would face ridicule or firing.

It got kicked up a hundred notches when we began to audition for the roles for the show. We easily found two wonderful drag queens to play two of the Belle sisters, but it proved quite difficult to find someone to play the main sister, named Jeza. After coming to the realization that there really was nobody perfect, I was filled with excitement and dread when I decided I would do something completely out of my wheelhouse and perform the role myself.

For one, I had never acted before. What if I totally sucked? Also, I'd never done drag before, outside of dressing for a party once. I had no earthly clue what I would be doing as an actor or a drag queen. But I knew it had to be me. It was not my original plan, but once it became clear, there really never was any other choice.

During preproduction, the team I was working with found an affordable and perfect location to shoot most of the scenes—and it happened to be two blocks away from my job. If I wasn't already scared shitless, rest assured now I had no need of a bowel movement whatsoever.

I went back and forth, over and over, about whether or not I should shoot the scenes. I was completely terrified that someone would notice me and I would lose my job. LGBTQ+ people lose their jobs for the littlest things in comparison to others, so walking down the street larger than life in hair that was bigger than most people just might put me in a more precarious employment position than most.

I prayed about writing the web series and found the strength to tell what I believed was an important story. I prayed about casting the parts and found the strength to realize I needed to assume this role. And I prayed about shooting the series and found the strength to get my big butt onto the streets of the neighborhood in full regalia, because the message of the story of humanity being saved by its cast-offs was too important to let fear box me in.

In 2 Corinthians 12, God says, "My power is made perfect in weakness". Drag queens are frankly the perfect vehicle of today's times for God to show that power. That is why I have, since the production of the web series, more than gladly embraced who I am and have become Jeza Belle.

Yes, the laughter and entertainment of my drag is so important for lifting the spirits of other people. But more importantly, I believe emphatically that God demonstrates his power through my drag because people see us drag queens as impaired, immoral beings.

I see drag queens as the best vehicles for Christ. Granted, this probably sets me apart from many people. But if makeup, ten tons of hair, flowing dresses, and being hilariously loud on both the inside and outside grab people's attention and lightens their loads, these things also can help them to look upward.

This is true again because my God moves through what others toss to the side. My God is the God of those who are being picketed against, twisting his own words to excuse vile and hate- fueled rhetoric. My God demonstrates his love through what some Christian believe are loveless beings.

That is the kind of strength that my God has and the type of strength that he gives to you and to me.

Through him, they can enact legislation to keep us from parades; they can gay-stomp our faces into the ground; they can refuse to bake us cakes or sign our marriage certificates; they can even dance on the graves of our brethren when they are gunned down and murdered for gathering at a gay bar. However, they cannot break our spirits—that power comes from God above and God alone, regardless of what they might write on a picket poster.

Gay, Lesbian, Bisexual, Transgender, Queer, Intersex, Asexual, Nonconforming, Two-Spirit, and anyone else I inadvertently left off this list. Whether you are a he, a she, or a they, *we* have power in God. *We* are worthy. Our strength comes from the infinite creator. We are strong because he is strong.

PRAYER

Lord and savior, please give me the strength to face all things, including those forces that work to block my path to your side. I know your power is made perfect in weakness, and so I ask you Lord to work through my weaknesses to demonstrate your wondrous power. I can do all things through

Christ who strengthens me, and I stand on these words because they are truth.

REFLECTION

1. Where in my life can God's strength be made perfect?

2. What are the parts of me that God can work through that might be considered unworkable by others, or even myself at times?

3. In which parts of my life do I need to lean on the Maker for greater strength to handle difficult situations, new beginnings, or stepping out on faith?

Guilt

"Therefore, there is now no condemnation for those
who are in Christ Jesus."

—ROMANS 8:1

The first time I had sex with another man that led to a bodily discharge, I had two distinct feelings. One was, why in the world did I wait so long for this incredible experience? The other was guilt.

We are conditioned from the time we are children to feel bad about anything that involves pleasure. It must be wrong if it feels so right. This is especially true when it comes to sex and sexuality. In many religious circles today, there is an ever-growing acceptance of gay marriage. However, even in these churches, it is sometimes counterbalanced by a pervasive viewpoint that while gays and lesbians in committed relationships akin to the marriage contract are acceptable, gay men and women who have sex outside of the marriage bed are still living in sin.

Realistically, I am not sure there exists any combination of human beings who do not engage in some type of sexual endeavor prior to marriage today. That is not to say people should not try to remain virgins, and I do not just mean vaginal or anal virgins, as many of these "virgins" to the marriage bed have been oral or tactile sex experts long before their vows, but that pure chastity prior to one's wedding is something rare at best.

As Christians, we do have a duty to try to be as good as we can as we walk through our lives, so that we are drawing a distinction between ourselves and the world and thus holding up the name of Christ. Yet, I do question if we have set the physical act of sex up to be more problematic than it actually was meant to be.

The bodies that God created have physical needs. These include the need to eat, to drink, to breathe, and I argue to engage in sexual release, be it for procreation or not. Ejaculation and orgasm are physical forces that the mind does not have the actual ability to completely stop the body from participating in.

If one does not hit that spot in the waking world, the body will take over and release during one's sleep. Hence, wet dreams. Let's face it, men and women alike are reaching sexual climax one way or another, because the body will not have it any other way.

As Israelites and followers of Yeshua, the Jewish people following the Law were forbidden from eating certain foods. Pork is the one that comes to most people's minds when thinking about what Jews could and could not eat, and this extended as far as to cover shellfish. I shudder today to think I would have to abstain from eating shrimp and lobster if we were still meant to follow the law to the T!

When Peter had a dream in the book of Acts, where all kinds of food came down from heaven and he was commanded to eat from what were forbidden items under Jewish law, his reaction was visceral.

"Surely not, Lord!" Peter replied. "I have never eaten anything impure or unclean." The voice spoke to him a second time, "Do not call anything impure that God has made clean" (Acts 11:8–9).

Peter walked away from his dream knowing that what Jews and Gentile ate was now and forever more irrelevant because God had opened the door to all people, regardless of the guilt associated with doing anything "impure" or "unclean," which included eating things that were up until that moment forbidden. It was a watershed moment in Christianity, where the message became clear: all were welcome.

Sex, no matter who it is with, falls into the same category as food in my mind. We all need it. Our bodies demand it. We do not stop eating even if we are a glutton, though we may choose to cut back and be more selective in our nutritional choices at various times in our lives, but we still are required by the flesh to eat.

Just as the Jewish law had the men of Peter's time working themselves up into Pharasiacial and Sadducean fits of propriety over what was clean and unclean to eat, we find the same behavior in many of today's leading evangelicals et. al. when it comes to sex. They flail and foment over what passes the lips or hips while their hearts are black as tar.

We are free from guilt because we are free through Christ.

This is not carte blanche to go out and be a ho, but it is carte blanche to let go of the guilt associated with having sex outside of marriage regardless of your preference. We likely should try to be discerning, just as we should try to eat the best we can, but the reality is, I eat like a pig, and sometimes I have sex like one too. Oink-oink.

One is not going to hell because one hooks up in the bathroom, their hotel room, or their own home with another human being. One is more prone to the fires if one treats people with ill intent, takes advantage of the weak, turns their backs on those in need, and recklessly uses the name of God to hurt rather than heal.

"Therefore, since we have been justified by faith, we have peace with God through our Lord Jesus Christ." (Romans 5:1).

Guilt can take on many forms beyond the molehill we somehow turn into the biggest of mountains. Guilt can involve living with the decisions we make.

When thieves broke into my sister's house last summer while she was present, she simply went to sleep rather than call 911. While she lived less than one minute from my parents, in fact on their same farm property in a house that you can see from their kitchen window, when the intruders physically broke the front door down right next to her bed, she saw no need to take any action other than to roll over.

Several years back, as I mentioned earlier, she had been diagnosed with white matter brain disease. All indications were that with certain lifestyle choices, the disease could be dramatically slowed down or potentially not advance any further. In fact, each time she went for tests, the brain looked relatively the same on the scans as the times before.

Yet, my sister's choices and actions began to get weirder and weirder. She had always been odd, but without an exact clinical diagnosis, we really went through life thinking she was a combination of both dippy and depressed. However, after the break-in, things began to rapidly deteriorate.

Yes, there were many warning signs in retrospect, but like anything, when you are too close to it, sometimes you don't see these changes taking place. It is like hair or nails growing. You do not notice their length until they are already too long.

After the break-in, my sister began falling over. One time, she walked outside, then rolled down a country hill, where she sat lying in a ditch for an hour until she was discovered. She could no longer use one of her hands because it shook so violently. You would ask her if she wanted milk in her cereal, and she would reply something like, "Yes, I am supposed to wear a yellow dress but the weather looks like a doughnut." Responses that were frankly from another planet.

We rapidly moved her into my parents' home, as it was no longer safe for her to be alone. But with my eighty-one-year-old father taking care of my mother post-brain surgery already, the living situation was unsustainable.

I live many hours away, in a fourth-floor walk-up in Manhattan, and I travel frequently. I would have gladly taken my sister in but for two facts. One, she could not physically get up or down the stairs to my apartment. Two, as I was often away, if she ever did come down the stairs and went outside without my knowledge, I would never see her again, as she no longer had the capacity to make any rational decisions, nor would she be able to find her way back upstairs. She would be lost, abducted, or worse.

Only months after moving in with my parents, she in a rapid sequence was rushed to the emergency room for various medical emergencies, where eventually they determined that she was in dire need of placement in a nursing home. However, due to her disability, her age, and her financial status, we were informed it was nearly impossible for her to receive the care she needed and that we should expect placement to take years.

Day after day, my sister sat in the hospital. She would have flashes of lucidity where she would beg me to take her home. Most of the time, though, she was no longer herself but rather a vacant being. It is a terrible thing to have to watch someone you love become hollow and deteriorate

Yet there was nowhere for her to go that would give her the full-time care she needed, my parents could not care for her, and we did not have the means to afford to pay privately for full- time, round-the-clock care. Sadly, the options for the sick are quite limited when you are not rolling in the big bucks.

Day after day, hour after hour, I prayed incessantly for intervention in a situation where it seemed there was no answer possible. I felt terribly guilty that I had to leave my sister in the hospital, but I also knew that the almost nonexistent chances for a nursing home placement would fully become a dead end if we moved her back home. She would only be back in the ER the next day.

Enter God.

After three weeks of wonderful care at the hospital, they called me up one day to say a mountain had been moved and a bed been assigned for my sister in a nursing home several hours away with the type of unit care she required.

I felt a mix of elated praise for God through whom I knew this blessing was delivered, and paralyzing guilt.

It was five days until the transfer took place, yet each of those days and the nights in between I spent in tears, feeling so bad that I was sending my sister off to a home. She is almost the same age as I am, and I felt like I was willfully abandoning her.

Unfortunately, my sister's eventually discovered diagnosis of leuko-dystrophy, beyond the white matter brain disease, is progressive. This rare condition will lead to both the eventual loss of all bodily and all mental function, including the abilities to walk, talk, see, and hear. It's a horrible future.

Knowing these facts, I still struggled with making the right decision without guilt. Yet, I found myself comforted by the words in 1 Peter 5:7: "Cast all your anxiety on him because he cares for you."

Guilt has no power over me because God can take over my worries and all of my feelings of indecision. My sister needed the care, God opened the door, and I did what I never thought I would be able to do and allowed her to be moved hours away from any family member to a home where they are providing her with the appropriate care twenty-four hours a day.

"For God did not send his Son into the world to condemn the world, but to save the world through him." (John 3:17)

We are freed from guilt and its soul-staining residue. God makes us clean before him, both in body and consciousness. Let us rejoice together in the lightness of being that comes with the lifting of all guilt and shame.

PRAYER

Jesus my savior has taken guilt and shame away from me, and for this I rejoice. For all of the things I have done that I feel bad and sorry about, I know they are gone through Christ's cleansing blood. May I turn my eyes toward love and justice and peace for others and not inward toward things that are already gone in your eyes, Lord. I am released, and I am clean before you.

REFLECTION

1. Where has guilt played a part in my life?

2. Are there things I am doing now that I feel compelled to do out of guilt and shame?

3. What can I release to God and no longer hold on to?

Persecution and Justice

"Blessed are those who are persecuted because of righteousness for theirs is the kingdom of heaven. Blessed are you when people insult you, persecute you and falsely say all kinds of evil against you because of me. Rejoice and be glad, because great is your reward in heaven, for in the same way they persecuted the prophets who were before you."

—MATTHEW 5:10–12

It is not popular or easy to be an LGBTQ+ Christian. On the right, you have those who try to block your path. On the left, you have those who have been harmed by so-called Christians and as such balk at your belief. One side believes you are unworthy. The other side believes you are unenlightened. Fear not, though—above everything is the all-knowing, all-powerful, all-loving God and his son, Jesus.

As a gay man, and a drag queen, I have faced much adversity. Some of the persecution, to be real though, happens from right within our own proud rainbow circles.

People in the gay community often joke about how they never really knew bullying until they came out and joined the gay world at large. In most cases, this has to do with the brutally extreme emphasis placed on physical appearance.

One can leave their hometown filled with pure excitement for life in the bigger cities, where a gaggle of gays walk the streets in every direction. Once there, though, many are disenchanted to find that unless their bodies have zero percent fat and they've been nipped, plucked, tucked, and styled within an inch of their lives, they are cast out of the mainstream quicker than they can announce their pronouns.

I have found myself often walking in between cliques. For one, I have been fat, skinny, marginally beautiful (my mother said so), and beat down but never really found much value in what exists on the surface. Now, that does not mean I do not like a good visual! I love me some hot men, and hot fun. But looks fade, and bodies sag, while spirits soar at all ages and body shapes.

As a Christian, and a Jewish Christian at that, finding safe spaces to discuss, reflect on, pray with, and study anything related to God can prove to be more challenging. For years, I searched unsuccessfully for a space that felt right in my own Christian journey.

Mainstream churches made it clear they did not want me. They saw me as the unclean thing lying on the side of the road that their religion forbade them from associating with. Everything centers for them on what looks good on the outside, and it would go against the grain to break bread, much less pray and praise God, with someone their ilk saw as immoral.

Within the LGBTQ+ community, though, I found an equal reaction, in that they leapt back in terror as if I had leprosy when they found out I was a practicing Christian who "still" believed in God. One cannot totally blame them when most of the ones I knew who grew up in churches have been so completely jacked up mentally and emotionally by other Christians that many have been suicidal and have had to spend years digging out of the self-hatred that came from years of religious teaching while growing up.

For many of them, the obvious conclusion was that God could not really exist, or at least they had no interest in hearing about the Christian God, whom they were led to believe hated them with a passion of fire and brimstone. So, they recoiled at my belief and called it brainwashing or a failing of modern intelligence.

Numerous friends whom I hold dear make constant posts online disparaging any belief in God or Christ. More than once, they have written in response to my posts about my own faith commenting on how ridiculous it is for me to believe God exists.

I was preparing to speak in drag at a church event several years ago when someone I knew sent me a message that said, "Are you kidding me? Do you actually believe in this fantastical crap?"

It is more than okay. I love them and frankly fully understand why the un-Christlike behavior of Christians over time would lead them to unbelief and hostility to my religious faith.

Yet here I am. A gay Christian. Well studied, and frankly well-aware of the chasm that has been created by the followers of my faith. If people who believe in God yet do not believe that homosexuals can be Christians assail me, and they do, I count that as something that puts me in the rare air of Jesus himself. If those in my own gay family blast me for proclaiming my faith in Christ, I wear that with pride, because I know that my redeemer lives.

If you are LGBTQ+ and believe in God; if you are an ally and believe that God is for all and loves all including homosexuals and transgender people; if you voice and stand up for those beliefs and share your faith and your story, you can expect to experience a lot of persecution. It may come at the hands of those farthest or at the hands of those nearest. Take heart, though, for Jesus said in John 15, "If they persecuted me, they will also persecute you."

There are other types of persecution beyond pushback for one's religious beliefs. In fact, LGBTQ+ people know mistreatment as well as, if not better than, most marginalized communities. Throughout history, our abuses have gone beyond being labeled, being forced to gather only in certain spaces with others of like kind, being taunted, and even being physically abused. Our persecutions have most often, in most societies, and in most points in history, led to death.

Unfortunately, the killing of LGBTQ+ people continues around the world today. In many countries it is not only illegal to be homosexual or transgender, and not only is that punishable by extremely dangerous prison sentences, but in far too many places around the globe still, being gay is a death sentence.

I have friends who have fled a number of African countries in particular, only to find themselves in refugee camps such as the one in Kakuma, Kenya. Here, men and women from around the continent enter spaces such as this one hoping to find safety while they remain onsite long enough to be legally transferred to safer, more permanent placements throughout the world.

However, having often barely escaped from their hometowns and countries with just their lives, LGBTQ+ refugees at camps like Kakuma are reportedly subject to horrendous abuses including assault, rape, and torture.

As both members of the LGBTQ+ community and as allies, it is incumbent upon us to do our best to not only help ourselves when we are persecuted, but also to stand up for others. Whether this is by providing for their basic needs or by fighting on their behalf when they have no voice.

"This is what the LORD says: Do what is just and right. Rescue from the hand of the oppressor the one who has been robbed. Do no wrong or violence to the foreigner, the fatherless or the widow, and do not shed innocent blood . . ." (Jeremiah 22:3)

Whether we or others face persecution at home or abroad for our sexuality, our gender identity, or anything else, God is on our side.

As 2 Thessalonians 1:6–7 says, "God is just: He will pay back trouble to those who trouble you and give relief to you who are troubled, and to us as well."

Therefore we must stand out in faith, we must "defend the weak and the fatherless; uphold the cause of the poor and the oppressed." (Psalms 82:3)

This is what justice is about at its core. God makes clear his stance on this. Jesus himself was the ultimate advocate for justice in this world. Today's Christians would piss themselves at Jesus's in-the-flesh actions around the critical and central importance of social justice.

He did not come to help the ones in power, or the rich, or the ones who were perceived to be the most holy. He came for everyone else, and to bring equity and equality across the board in his name. And because of this, he was persecuted, and you will be too whenever and wherever you stand up for what is right, especially in his name.

As a gay drag queen, I stand up in the name of Jesus against those who use his name to tear down the unprotected and the weak. I think we can all accept that if we do not fit into "the" box we can expect pushback from those within.

Rest assured, we and others who share the good message to all, including and especially to the LGBTQ+ community, will be persecuted in the name of Christ. Know this, though—God and the powerful social equalizing love of Jesus are on our side.

PRAYER

Give me the courage to stand up for what is right. To do what is often unpopular and do it because it is the right thing to do. You are a God of the weak and oppressed. May my life imitate those aspects of your being by being a voice for the voiceless and a shelter for the homeless. Help, Lord, find ways to bring justice and security to those without.

REFLECTION

1. Where in my life can I stand up for those who need help?

2. Which causes do I see as the most Christlike, where Jesus himself would take a stand?

3. What are the issues and causes that are most important to me? How can I make a difference in these areas?

4. How will I participate in social justice movements?

Joy

God did not place us here to be party poopers. We equate Christians with sour lemons. Joy is central to the human and creator-endowed experience. This goes beyond laughter—it goes to the spirit within that radiates from a life of freedom that is infinitely connected to the hope we have both in this world and the next.

A song from my youth that comes directly from Philippians 4:4 dances in my head frequently. It simply repeats the verse *"Rejoice in the Lord always, and again I say rejoice."* Pretty simple, but the message is unmistakably clear—keep joy at the forefront of your being, because the Lord has got you in his hand.

Even in the darkest of times, joy permeates the Christian's being because it is rooted in our hope. In fact, those words about rejoicing were written while Paul was in prison in Rome. In all things and at all times, we can find a reason to rejoice, because we have God near us. If that is not worth rejoicing over, nothing in this world is.

In Psalms, people danced in the streets and played instruments repeatedly in joyful celebration for the lives God gave them.

In 1 Corinthians 10:31, we were commanded, "whether you eat or drink or whatever you do, do it all for the glory of God."

Anyone who tells you that you cannot be joyful as a follower of God either knows nothing of him or needs to pull the stick out of their backside.

The joy that I want to focus more deeply on here, though, goes beyond happiness. Rather, it is a contentment that radiates from within.

As a wise Sicilian old lady in Miami once said, "Picture it- Persia. The year is 445 BC..." Nehemiah is a cupbearer for the Persian king. When the Jews return to Jerusalem after the Babylonian exile, Nehemiah travels back to the city to help oversee the rebuilding of the city's walls. Subsequently, he finds that many of the Jews are not following God's laws, are being mean spirited to the poor and weak, and are intermingling with the Gentiles so as to not place God at the forefront of their existence once again.

Nehemiah forces the Jewish nobles to cancel all debts to the poor, and when the walls are finally completed, he has Ezra read the law of Moses to all of the Jewish people assembled, where they began crying and wailing when they hear God's words, which pierce their souls. In turn, Nehemiah says to them, "Go and enjoy choice food and sweet drinks, and send some to those who have nothing prepared. This day is holy to our Lord. Do not grieve, for the joy of the Lord is your strength." (Nehemiah 8:10)

Now, Nehemiah could have easily told them they were right to cry and that they should do much more because they were wicked, hard-necked people who repeatedly called on God to do things for them, then once he did, they turned their backs to him again and again. Instead, he told them not to cry because "the joy of the Lord" was their strength.

True joy is a sense of completeness from a deep and abiding relationship with God. So much so that one struggles to put into words what that feeling actually constitutes, but when you feel it, it is like skydiving and meditation at the same time.

I remember clearly the day I was baptized. I was twelve or thirteen years old and had been a devout believer in Christ as the Messiah and God as my Father already for many years. Odd to think that such a complete knowledge of God's existence and Jesus's role as savior was with me from as far back as I can remember, but it has always been so for me. As such, I have always had an enormous gut full of devotion and love for my Lord and savior. It can almost feel funny saying it to others at times because it is so intimate and so innate that whenever I do discuss it, I'm really delving into my deepest core as a being and that can feel quite scary. It can also feel quite joyful to share what I know to be so.

Back to the baptism. I believed for years but had finally reached an age where my parents agreed it was okay to go ahead with this act, though I had been asking for ages.

There is much debate across all spectrums of Christianity around baptism. Who should do it, when should it happen, how should it be done. I am not going to spend my time here parsing the different beliefs and rationales. The older I get, the more I believe these kinds of arguments are wasted moments that should be given over by us to more important matters.

In the church I grew up in, there was a strong belief in baptism by immersion when one was old enough to make a conscious decision with full understanding about who Jesus was, about the remission of sins that the full immersion in water represents, and about what it meant to take on the mantle of a Christian who would rise up from the water filled with the Holy Spirit.

When the day came, I remember walking my skinny little butt out into the water in the baptismal font. The minister asked me if I believed that Jesus was the Son of God, and I answered yes. He then declared that he was baptizing me in the name of the Father, the Son, and the Holy Spirit for the remission of my sins.

As he submerged my body completely under the water, I rose up filled with the most inexplicable feeling, as I touched on earlier. I had never before nor never since known such an elation of the body and soul, because I had a perfect union with my Lord.

Joy is comfort to the soul at all levels. It might come in the form of laughter, it might come in the form of contented peace, but however it comes, it is an important part of our lives, and God expects us to bathe ourselves in a joyful existence.

One need not be in a constant fit of religious ecstasy such as a baptism to feel joy. It can exist on a stage when you are making others laugh or take notice of your skills. I'm speaking here of others, as my skills on stage are questionable at best. There are some queens who go out and bust a move that makes your head spin as far and as hard as their hips do. That's joy!

Whatever form you find it in, embrace it, because God has given you life to live. As is written in Ecclesiastes, "There is nothing better for a person under the sun than to eat and drink and be glad." So, do so, in whatever form makes you the most fulfilled.

PRAYER

Father, you made today, and I will rejoice and be glad in it. May I find deep fulfillment, and a love of all things on this day because of you. As I am filled up by you, may I fill the cups of others.

REFLECTION

1. Where do I find joy in my life?

2. In what ways have I been blessed in positive, uplifting ways?

3. How can I spread the joy that I have in my heart to other people? Is there something I can commit to doing today, small or big?

Love the Sinner, Hate the Sin

"Truly I tell you, people can be forgiven all their sins and every slander they utter, but whoever blasphemes against the Holy Spirit will never be forgiven; they are guilty of an eternal sin."

—MARK 3:28–30

We are all sinners. It is one of the most fundamental premises of Judeo-Christianity. One does not need to be either Jewish or Christian to know deep down in our bones it is true. Some people posit that Christianity does not square with modern thought because it is an upward-facing faith that counters our contemporary obsession with self-worth and self-empowerment. To them, Christianity is an antiquated belief system born out of mankind's uneducated fears and a need to blame the unknown world on the supernatural. Yet no person alive would likely even attempt to counter the idea that as human beings, we all do things that are considered wrong at various points in our lives.

Let us face it—at times, each of us are envious; we hate, even if we try our hardest not to; we have flashes of anger; we drop a lie here and there; we see people in need and are unmoved; and we all live for some freshly served, piping-hot tea. The Bible makes clear that there are a whole host of things that are either universally or contextually sinful. It's not that unmodern after all.

Christianity closed the circle on ancient Judaism, which put forth a system by which spilling the blood of animals would cover over the sins of people before their God. God being holy, Jews needed to constantly restitute for their sins through spilt blood in order to make them clean and able to continue to come before him in this relationship, and as such, it was a system that required constant sacrifice.

When Jesus died, his spilt blood, being both human and divine, became the last and purest blood sacrifice needed. His perfect sacrifice brought the need for future sacrifice to a close, as followers had both their past and future sins washed away. They were free to enter into a constant state of communion with God, as Jesus made them clean before the Father.

This does not mean that followers of Jesus do not sin. It means followers of Jesus sin, but because of their belief, their baptism into that belief, these sins remain atoned for.

Equally, because of that permanent atonement, it does not mean that Christians are expected to, or should, run out and go buck wild and do anything sinful under the sun. It means that because we are all in a constant state of imperfection, Jesus has us covered.

Once we get over the minor hump that we are all sinful, the debate fans out into an argument over degrees of sin, especially for today's Christians.

Many modern evangelicals spend an extraordinary amount of energy seeking to vilify and block off people from any activities they deem as more sinful on their weighted list of wrongdoings. They spend their time entering themselves into the political arena, working to put into place laws that dip into the lives and actions of others, and going forth with little to no moral authority to denounce the deeds of other people, while seldom to never looking at how unaligned with the teachings of Christ their actions are.

The Jewish Messiah was expected to come as a political and national war hero to the Jews who had been awaiting his entrance onto the world stage for millennia. There was a false expectation that he would fight back physically and politically against the global forces of whichever era he sprang forth into the world during. Yet, when he finally arrived, he did not dip even a pinky into politics, national identity, or the debate over codified legal issues, beyond those strictly connected to the religious laws that he himself was at the center of.

In fact, when asked about paying Roman taxes, a modern political debate of importance to the religious at the time, Jesus put it right back onto the Pharisees and told them to give Caesar back the coins with his face on them per their unimportant tax laws, but more importantly, focus their attention not on the national and local political issues of the day but on giving to God what is his; our hearts, minds, souls, and strength. Local and national politics meant absolutely nothing to Christ.

When looking at this in the context of today, one can't help but picture Jesus telling conservative Christians to get their noses out of national and local politics and into giving to God what is his. If we are giving God what is his, that involves our spreading the gospel of light, not spending untold time and riches trying to limit what is taught in AP Biology via state legislatures or creating congressional laws that determine who can receive gender-affirming care. These acts are not doing God's work or giving God what is his. Instead, these acts are more like sin than the very things they claim to fight against on God's behalf.

What is really more sinful? Is it a man sleeping with another man, or is it wasting millions of dollars on state propositions to block same-sex marriage that could instead feed and clothe the homeless in the name of the God you claim to follow?

Is it more sinful to drink at a lesbian bar or to tear down another's soul with hateful words

Is it more sinful for a man to wear a dress or for a man to not love his neighbor as himself?

In both Matthew and Mark, Jesus said that there was one sin that rose above all of the rest, one that was unforgivable. That sin was blaspheming the Holy Spirit. To many, the definition of blaspheming the Spirit involves refusing God, hardening one's heart to him over time despite repeatedly being shown his power, and refusing to repent in the name of Christ.

Jesus did not say homosexual sex, being transgender, or dressing in drag were unforgivable sins. He didn't even say these were sins at all. For heaven's sake then, it is anyone's guess why supposed Christians spend so much fecking time on these BS issues. As a Christian too, I will tell you, the acknowledgment of Christ and repentance for all of the mess we are is what makes us whole, and that is what the message of the Gospel is about. It is not about rating sins, because we all have them. We all do them. It is repenting of these sins, the main one being our unbelief. Refusing to acknowledge that sin before God is what ultimately becomes unforgivable; everything and anything else, God will work with.

When someone uses the popular expression "love the sinner; hate the sin," I am always torn between either laughing in their faces or hugging them, because in the deepest recesses of my being, I know that they are the sinners. Poor deluded souls that are unable to see the giant hypocrite logs jammed into their own eyeballs.

I am reminded of an image from a few years back of a drag queen at a Pride parade in California. "Christians" with anti-LGBT signs were on the sidelines of the parade yelling nasty things to the marchers. This drag queen went over and stood up and over them. A picture was snapped by the press of this man in woman's clothes who was face-to-face with people misusing the name of Christ to spew hate. This image cuts right to the heart of the sin debate. Did Jesus, or even the apostles, at any time run around Jerusalem with signs getting in the faces of the masses telling them they were going to hell? Poor, deluded, miseducated, and un-Christlike fools.

Let us hate their hatred but love these lost beings. May their souls find true peace in Christ.

Anyone who knows me knows that I am a great follower of American politics. For the most part, my fascination comes from the constant attempt by the religious to shove morality down the throats of others. Thus, I tend to rant quite a bit online about these politically conservative morons, because I find them so loathsomely anti-God.

My rants for the last number of years have centered frequently on that of one particular former president, because his emergence on the political scene seemed to let loose and give permission to the most hateful beliefs to come out from the shadows with some kind of sick legitimacy.

No person and their followers could possibly encapsulate my feelings for "love the sinner, hate the sin" more than Donald Trump and his MAGA crowd. They epitomize sin on so many levels.

Megalomania, racism, loathing toward immigrants, wasted time and breath on acts of hatred. On every level, their beliefs and actions swing wildly in the opposite direction from the teachings of Christ. They got the sin and sinner part of the phrase down pat! They own those to the core. Yet for as much as many would believe that I despise Trump—and he does take me quite to the edge of my Christian love—I would sit down at a table with him today. It's about loving them in spite of their darkness and demonic dispositions.

Most of my friends and followers would be beyond shocked to know that despite all he has done to hurt so many, I would forgive Donald Trump in a nanosecond if he had a spiritual Road to Damascus, a "come to Jesus moment" himself the way Paul did.

I'd even break bread with many of our political leaders, even though to me many of them act as if they are starring as the grand-dame-epic-twats of a national telenovela. If Donald Trump and any of his wacky followers including those American-Political- Christians and pseudo-evangelicals repented of their sin of using God's name to inflame hatred, I would embrace them today the way God embraced me despite all of my failings.

After all, I do love all sinners just like Jesus, and we as Christians are all called to do the same.

PRAYER

Grant me the strength of Jesus to love those who persecute others, who persecute me, and who make life difficult for so many innocents by falsely using your name to further their earthly aims. I pray that each of these people find peace and turn to you and others with love. I pray I will also welcome these people with open arms, as we all fall short of your glory, Lord.

REFLECTION

1. Who are the people I have the most difficulty loving?

2. What is sin? Where do I find it in my life and the lives of those I have difficulty dealing with?

3. How could lifting these people up in prayer be helpful for both themselves and for me?

4. Are there people close to me whom I need to make a more conscious effort to love despite their flaws and mistakes?

Gender and Gender Identity

"So God created mankind in his own image, in the image of God he
created them; male and female he created them."

—(GENESIS 1:37)

Gender identity is currently a flash point in American Christianity. A few men, many of whom probably secretly put on their wives or girlfriend's panties, have made everything from clothing, to pronouns, to medical transitioning, to drag queen book readings at libraries into a central focus for the American evangelical political movement.

There is so much that can be said about gender and the Bible, but let us start with the beginning of the beginning. In the first pages of the bible, a woman, Eve, is theoretically birthed from the body of a man, Adam. Basically, the story of humans opens immediately with a curveball that from the very first moments of time demonstrates that gender and its norms are immediately fluid.

Thousands of years later, we stand here arguing over the "natural order" of things, when natural in human's dawn of existence was the man giving physical life to another being, not a woman pushing an infant out of her cooch. It wasn't until the fall of man in the Garden later on, when woman was cursed to labor pains, that women were even to become the givers of life.

Post Garden of Eden, and throughout the rest of the Bible, we see two things play out that many people today who fall all over themselves about the issue of gender basically ignore. These two issues include the roles of men and women and a running subtext of the Lord using women in roles that were supposed to be afforded only to men whenever it fell outside of the context of separation from the nonbelievers.

In the context of the times, many laws and rules were instituted about man and woman to demonstrate the separation of the Jews from the Gentiles. For example, in Deuteronomy, the law is laid down that "a woman must not wear men's clothing, nor a man wear women's clothing, for the Lord your God detests anyone who does this" (22:5). Many biblical scholars agree that this law was in direct reference to the nearby local Gentiles' practice of worshipping their gods with a ceremony whereby the women dressed as soldiers and the men donned the women's clothes. It was a narrow reference to what was distinctly relevant to the lives of the people whom the law was handed down to at the time. Yet today, this verse is repeatedly cited to justify hatred against transgender, gender nonconforming, and other individuals. One can't help but chuckle at how convenient it is that pants are acceptable for evangelical women in today's times but men in frocks are not.

Alongside the laws in the Torah that separated the Jews from the Gentiles, we find women throughout the Bible elevated to positions that men, then and now, claimed as sacrosanct to the God-ordained separation of the sexes. The prophetess Deborah and a Kenite woman named Jael come immediately to mind.

In the book of Judges, chapter four, a prophet woman named Deborah was leading Israel at the time. We need to let that sink in. For all the talk of woman's place beneath man, for all the men who starred in the story of the Israelites thus far, a woman was leading God's people—and not only as a prophetess for her direct communication with God, but as a judge of disputes between the Israelite people. You know, just going about her God-ordained life thousands of years ago, doing what humans have consistently coined a man's job.

Deborah tells a man named Barak that he is to take an army and free the Israelites from a king of Canaan and his army's commander, Sisera. When the clash takes place, Sisera flees and ultimately falls asleep in a tent, where a woman named Jael drives a tent stake through his head as he lay sleeping.

Wonder women having been bending the rules of gender with God's consent and approval for eons.

"Youth oppress my people, women rule over them." (Isaiah 3:12)

Evangelicals today use this quote in Isaiah to build an argument that God only used Deborah and Jael to shame men for their lack of faith, that they were an anomaly to prompt men never to be so weak as to have women need to step in again. Thus, they attempt to reclaim authority and piss in the ground to remark their territorial lines that they insist must exist between the sexes.

Yet for me personally, they strengthen my own argument for my quest to use drag to inspire people to look to God. If the Lord used women to shame men for their lack of religious faith, then may my wearing women's clothing shame them for their lack of Christianity today. If a man in drag is so shameful, then they should truly fall on their faces and dress themselves in sackcloth and ashes, because most of the drag queens I know demonstrate more attributes of Christ and his teachings than a gigantic portion of American church congregants. #Facts

Galatians 3:28 makes it perfectly clear that there is no male or female in Christianity. You are either a Christian or you are not. Penises and vaginas hold no power here. So, if there is no male or female, then the argument over transgender people is moot as well. It is not existent, as sex and gender are nonexistent ideas in Christianity.

Yes, I am certain one will quote Ephesians 5:22 that says wives should submit to their husbands as an excuse for gender guardrails whereby we have two sexes, with one leading the other. I am not personally sure that this verse doesn't have more to do with relationships as a whole and the way we need to treat each other in our partnerships versus a declarative declassing of women for all of eternity.

I have already mentioned how the natural world God created has numerous creatures that defy gender and even change gender. It is the way the infinite Father created this awe-inspiring world. If he created critters on land and sea that could change genders, then he certainly is not as uptight and rigid about gender transitioning as the screaming-mimis of conservative religious sects of today.

Jesus himself talks about eunuchs, the gender-benders of his time, by saying, "For there are eunuchs who were born that way, and there are eunuchs who have been made eunuchs by others—and there are those who choose to live like eunuchs for the sake of the kingdom of heaven. The one who can accept this should accept it." (Matthew 19:12). For goodness' sake, if the savior tells you to get over it, then get the F over it!

This narrative of equality continues when an Ethiopian eunuch is one of the first people baptized into the Christian faith in Acts 8. In fact, Philip is led in the direction he is told to go by an angel of God. Any Christian who takes issue with gender identity and gender expression being permitted by God needs to call his angel and the apostle Philip on whichever app works best for them.

God does not ultimately give a rat's patoot if someone is born with male sex organs but changes them to female sex organs. He does not care if a man puts on a gallon of makeup. It matters not if a woman wears a pair of jeans, nor if a person is fluid and does not fit neatly into a gender box. None of these things have anything whatsoever to do with the central tenets of Christianity.

Genesis is a beautiful transgender woman who attends a local church. She is devoted to God and tries her best to live a quiet, Christian life. Tammy is a transgender woman who is a full-time nurse. She spends her days taking care of the sick. Both women seek to build people up and walk around with love in their hearts that they freely share with others.

There is not enough paper to print all of the good deeds drag kings and drag queens do for charities. Every day of every week, there are multiple performances taking place around the world specifically to raise funds for those who are ill, to feed and clothe those who are without, and to help the oppressed, whatever those needs might be.

Once again, Jesus himself said it best. "Likewise, every good tree bears good fruit, but a bad tree bears bad fruit." (Matthew 7:17)

I will take a wonderful and beautiful soul whose outside packaging may have changed to better fit who they are on the inside any day over someone who clings to rigid gender norms but has no love in their hearts. I believe God will too.

PRAYER

Heavenly Father, there is no male or female in Christ, as your own word stated. Thank you for freeing me from the burden of limitations that others seek to place onto me. May I focus my days on bearing good fruit in your name, and waste little energy or time on those too myopic to see your wonder works through souls, and is not dependent on pronouns, testosterone, estrogen, or reproductive organs.

REFLECTION

1. What are my beliefs about gender norms?

2. How do I feel about gender expression, gender fluidity, and God's position on these?

3. Where do gender and identity fall on a list of what is most important to God? Why?

PRIDE = Self-Worth

"For you created my inmost being; you knit me together in my mother's womb. I praise you because I am fearfully and wonderfully made; your works are wonderful, I know that full well."

PSALMS 139:13–14

Every June, gay pride flags unfurl across the United States and many other countries. LGBTQ+ people in all their colorful glory take to the streets for marches and parades; businesses tout the spending power of our community and prominently feature us in ads; political, sports, arts, and music heroes hail the rainbow nation; and conservative-Christians of all stripes lose their minds in what they claim to be is the name of Christ.

Recently, I was reading a random church's website that featured what they considered to be a forceful biblical pushback against gay pride. Their main argument? That the gay community had stolen the rainbow from Noah and hence was corrupt and morally repugnant. The crux of their counterculture argument boiled down to the fact that the LGBTQ+ community chose a flag that dared use the ROYGBIV spectrum of colors.

Not that incredibly inspiring of an argument, much less based on anything having to do with God, nor was it ultimately too convincing.

Another site featured a prominent pastor who claimed that in Mark 7:20–23, Jesus came out forcefully against homosexuality, though Jesus never used the actual word homosexuality or described homosexual acts.

"What comes out of a person is what defiles them. For it is from within, out of a person's heart, that evil thoughts come—sexual immorality, theft, murder, adultery, greed, malice, deceit, lewdness, envy, slander, arrogance and folly. All these evils come from inside and defile a person."

I find it ironic that the pastor began and ended on sexual immorality, which he alone aligned to homosexuality, but never made it to the end of Jesus's quote. After all, with his own self-selected passage, he damned most of the evangelical movement that emphatically lives in the space of malice, slander, arrogance, and folly. I suppose Jesus never meant that they could do any wrong? Only drag queens, women who sleep together, and men who marry other men.

Further, the pastor omitted that this whole chapter in Mark is basically Jesus going TF off on the Pharisees, whom many of our modern-day pseudo-Christians mirror. Jesus goes as far as to quote Isaiah at them: "These people honor me with their lips, but their hearts are far from me. They worship me in vain; their teachings are merely human rules." (Mark 7:6–7).

In other words, they spend all their lives following the law, building laws around the law, and making public spectacles of themselves over the law, but missing the heart of God's teachings altogether. Sounds like Pride Month panic to me.

Finally, anti-LGBTQ+ Christians most often simply rattle off a bunch of Bible quotes about man's pride during Pride Month, such as, "Pride goeth before destruction, and an haughty spirit before a fall." (Proverbs 16:18) Yet they demonstrate their complete ignorance on what LGBTQ+ pride and the month it is celebrated in actually mean.

Gay Pride, as it is most often called, at its core is not really about being proud as in arrogant or disdainful, it's about recognizing that LGBTQ+ people have worth. We are of value and refuse to be ignored, harmed, and treated like booboo anymore. That's not pride in the biblical sense, that's fighting back against the human pride of putting oneself above God by condemning others to hell. Finding love and worth in this space where we are constantly bombarded with extreme hatred from wolves in God's clothing is not only commendable, it is positively Christian.

The first Pride parade I attended was with my oldest brother. It was many years since I had left the church I had grown up in. However, as I spent so much of my time during the first few years of supposed freedom navel-gazing and trying to find balance in my relationship with God now that I was no longer in the fold, according to my former congregants, I more or less was oblivious to the entire gay world.

As such, when I arrived at a pier party with my brother, his partner, and some friends, I honestly was shocked to find that people could be happy and open with who they were as gay men and women. Seeing transgender, bisexual, and homosexual people, whom I had only seen and heard torn to shreds my entire life, walk around with their heads held high and demonstrate an ownership of their value as humans was transformative.

You mean I had worth too?

It all seemed to click. I had been beating myself up for failing as a Christian to stay the course, though I knew I was miserable before, pretending to be straight and denying myself a full life. Why couldn't I be Christian *and* gay? I started to realize that it was not God but people who were forcing me to choose one lane or the other.

That understanding brought enormous relief. I exhaled and found the voice within that I had been seeking since exiting the only church I had ever known. God was with me always and everywhere. He valued me, and I in turn did him a grave disservice by not fully valuing myself up to this point.

Sure, I had walked around looking like I was at peace from the outsider's perspective, but on the inside, it was no easy road those first few years. I stayed close to God but had a very difficult time with my fellow man. Their words would often swirl in my head that I was now lost. I knew I was not "lost" in the way they stated on one level, yet I felt so lost on another level altogether.

Over the years, I have found great joy during Pride month because I enjoy watching others embrace and love who they are. For me, as an LGBTQ+ Christian, as a performer, as a gay man, my pride is based on the fact that God loves me and has empowered me to do the same.

"We love because he first loved us." (1 John 4:19)

"Have I not commanded you? Be strong and courageous. Do not be afraid; do not be discouraged, for the Lord your God will be with you wherever you go." (Joshua 1:19)

God created me, and therefore I am proud of the person he made. Though I am weak, I am wonderfully made. I am courageous and strong, because how can one whom the Father has made and the Son has died for *not* live out loud?

Per both Galatians and 1 Corinthians, I am not boastful solely in myself, I am boastful in Christ Jesus.

At long last, I am here, I am queer, and God and I are *both* used to it!

PRAYER

Release me from self-hatred, Lord. Help me to be proud of who I am no matter what my sexual preference is, no matter what my gender or gender identity may be, and no matter what physical parts are attached to my outer being. Let me grab hold of the great empowerment that comes with knowing that I am loved by you God and your Son, who gave his life so that I can have a full and wonderful life both here and into eternity.

REFLECTION

1. At which times in my life did I feel the most proud of who I truly am on the inside?

2. Am I proud of who I am as a member of the LGBTQ+ community? Why or why not?

3. How can I be an ally, or a better ally, to LGBTQ+ people who often need support in loving who they are?

Abundance

"The thief cometh not but for to steal, and to kill, and to destroy. I am come that they may have life and that they may have it more abundantly."

—JOHN 10:10 (KJV)

When I was still in the closet, trying to force a square peg in a round hole by pretending, even to myself, to be straight, it was mentally and emotionally painful. There were times that all of the denial, the pushing down of who I really was deep inside of myself, found ways to bubble up and manifest that pain in other ways.

For a period of time after I left the church I grew up in, I became bulimic. I would eat vociferously anything and everything in sight, like a giant Hoover vacuum. Most often, I would do this binging in secret, where no one could see me. Miserably, I would consume excessive calories in private until my little stomach was near to burst. I would then follow that up with a trip to the bathroom, where I would put my finger down my throat and throw my guts up.

Something inside of me felt gross, like it needed to be excised from my body. Throwing up became symbolic of a last attempt to release from within me this demon I must have had, because no matter how hard I had tried in life, I was still gay. Why would it not come out of me?

I punished myself with binges of food and private purges over the toilet, hoping to rid myself of that part of me that was disgusting, not pure in the eyes of God, as I had heard my brethren tell me and others so often.

This was not abundant living.

I faked my feelings and pretended in front of others for years, and that was not abundant living either.

I could not rid myself of who I was, nor could I just live a normal life accepting who I was and being accepted by others.

Damn! The pressure of trying to constantly hide from yourself and others was exhausting. Who was I kidding, though? Certainly not God. He knew exactly who I was, and his Son even said he came so I could live my life abundantly, but here I was at various stages, a miserable wretch.

Many people I've known over the years lost the love and support of their families once they finally embraced who they were and stopped lying about it. Apparently, the lives of their family members were more abundant and fulfilled so long as my LGBTQ+ friend's lives were not.

For example, at the college I attended, whenever someone was outed, or even when someone whispered that another person was gay or lesbian to the right people, those individuals were brought before both a person of authority, such as a dean, and a psychologist. In most cases, these students who were named, as if they were witches in Salem, were given two choices. Immediate expulsion or conversion therapy in the form of one-on-one counseling to treat them psychologically in an effort to suppress or remove entirely the "disorder" of homosexuality from these matriculated students.

I remember so many years of presenting as happy to others in the Christian faith but feeling so sad that I was forever bound to a lie. I would never fully experience joy, while those around me who were not LGBTQ+ would have lives that were complete. Filled with love, even. People would fawn over the young couples at socials who held hands and kissed. Oh, youth!

Meanwhile, those of us who longed to do the same but with whom we were actually attracted to would simply have to smile along on the outside, while crying on the inside over our lives denied. Denied because others of this world demanded it to be so.

To this day, many of the men and women I know who went through such brutalized treatment such as conversion therapy or expulsion suffer from debilitating psychological effects. Even those who never had to experience the outings and forced counseling were scarred for life because of the constant guillotine of being named that dangled precariously above their necks for so long. What if they were outed? Would they lose their placement at the college? Worse, would their relationships with their family and friends end once the truth came out that they were gay?

These fears led, and likely continue to this day to lead, really wonderful people to become damaged, all because they want to follow Jesus but they are told by men that they must live narrow and miserable lives to do so.

How much more effective would it have been if instead of treating these young men and women like repugnant moral pariahs, they were treated like valuable, wonderful, God-created beings?

What if they were shown love and encouraged to live their lives abundantly in Christ because they were important to him, and therefore they were vital members of his church?

I was asked once to come speak at a church in the West Village in New York City on the topic of embracing who we are as LGBTQ+ Christians. It was the first, not last, time I was to physically speak in a church building dressed in drag. As I entered the sanctuary, I had a mini moment of panic, like "what in the world am I doing going into a church dressed like this?" Pure terror got my knees a-knocking.

Then, in my mind, I could hear these words: "For where two or three gather in my name, there am I with them." (Matthew 18:20)

Here awaiting me was a group of LGBTQ+ Christians, nonbelievers whose souls were seeking, as well as numerous straight allies of the faith who were wanting to hear a message of inclusion. That was what was important, not whether or not one of those gathered was wearing hooker heels. So I pulled my big britches up, otherwise known as spanx, lifted the hem of my dress, which incidentally was in a fabulous cow print, and walked my big behind up to the podium that sat in front of the pews.

I looked out and saw before me the most beautiful and diverse audience, ready to receive a message on the inclusivity of Christ. My cow knees stopped shaking, and all of my fear evaporated, leaving an overwhelming feeling of love, hope, and joy.

A building is a building, and no more or no less filled with God's presence whatever the sign on the marquee may say or what the decor may evoke. Here were just people, wanting to hear how the good news of the Gospel impacted my life as a Christian who just so happens to be gay and entertains in drag. I cannot think of another thing in this world that could be more fulfilling than sharing how God and Jesus have filled me up. Because he lives, my cup, as it were, runneth over. I am incredibly rich.

Over the years, I have learned to cast a wary eye on anyone who tries to limit the overflowing joy in my life because of their misguided beliefs.

God has blessed me in so many ways. He gave me a wonderful and loving husband that he hand-selected for me, a God-fearing man who shares the same value and belief system as I do. I have an amazing (and crazy) family that for the most part spends little time on whom I love and more time on the love we have for each other. Most importantly, though, I am secure in that I am covered in this life and the next because of my relationship with God and my full belief in the power of the cross and Jesus Christ. That's where my fullness comes from the most. All of the blessings of this temporal world will pass away, but my spirit through God will live on forever. That is life abundant!

LGBTQ+ people should live their lives out loud. We are his church. Jesus did not come to dampen our light and take away our joy, but rather to bring it to new heights.

PRAYER

Jesus came so that I may live an abundant life. God, please help me honor all of the abundance that is in my life right now, at this moment.

REFLECTION

1. Where is God's abundance evident in my life?
2. What are the stumbling blocks to abundance in my life?
3. How can I work to minimize these and maximize the fullness of being?

Stand Firm

"Finally, be strong in the Lord and in his mighty power. Put on the full armor of God, so that you can take your stand against the devil's schemes. For our struggle is not against flesh and blood, but against the rulers, against the authorities, against the powers of this dark world and against the spiritual forces of evil in the heavenly realms. Therefore put on the full armor of God, so that when the day of evil comes, you may be able to stand your ground, and after you have done everything, to stand. Stand firm then, with the belt of truth buckled around your waist, with the breastplate of righteousness in place, and with your feet fitted with the readiness that comes from the gospel of peace. In addition to all this, take up the shield of faith, with which you can extinguish all the flaming arrows of the evil one. Take the helmet of salvation and the sword of the Spirit, which is the word of God."

—EPHESIANS 6:10–17

Out of all the passages in the Bible, I suspect that this is the absolute last piece of scripture that American-Political-Christians, evangelicals, or conservative rabble rousers who incorrectly claim the name of Christ around the world would expect a big-haired, high-heel-wearing, married-to- another-man, straps-on-fake-boobs, gay drag queen to close out her/his/their spiritual memoir and devotional book with. To most of them, I am the very thing they must stand firm against.

Yet these words contain the force of our heavenly creator, who is on our side, and as Christians—yes even gay, lesbian, bisexual, transgender, queer, intersex, asexual, gender nonconforming, and/or pansexual Christians—these are our heirlooms and our birthright in Jesus to take hold of and wield. Perhaps even more so than for others, as we are in full need of that armor because of the slings and arrows that come our way come from all directions, including and extensively from within the Christian faith.

When an interview I had participated in regarding an LGBTQ+ Christian event taking place in New York City dropped in an American publication a number of years back, someone came for me with vitriol that was dipped in the devil's poison. This "Christian" lobbed bombs at me for daring to believe and proclaim that God would have anything to do with me as a drag queen and as a gay male. They concluded their tirade by assigning me to hell. I was not fazed or moved by their words, which sought to move or remove me from my place in Christ's fold then, and neither would I be so now.

As a Christian—and I am this before I am anything else in this world, as is anyone else once they embrace Jesus as savior—I have been given a full set of weaponry to withstand any assault that comes to interfere with the message of hope and the salvation that has been given to us in Jesus Christ. As have you.

Evil is not merely a list of bad things like drinking and gambling, or even being homosexual or transgender, that people use to separate the wheat from the chaff in churches. Evil is anything that tries to separate us from the love of God. For LGBTQ+ people, including those either seeking to know Christ or those already following him, that evil is too frequently evidenced in the words and deeds of other Christians themselves. Anyone who throws up a roadblock to another person knowing who Christ really is and who he really came for and why becomes a tool for "spiritual forces of evil in the heavenly realm." Ultimately, their words and their deeds hold no power over God and therefore no power over us.

"For I am persuaded that neither death, nor life, nor angels, nor principalities, nor powers, nor things present, nor things to come, nor height, nor depth, nor any other creature, shall be able to separate us from the love of God, which is in Christ Jesus our Lord." (Romans 8:38–39 KJV)

Anyone, including someone who believes themselves to be a practicing Christian, whose intent is to separate us from that love is doing the work of Satan, not Christ.

Let me say that again for the back row—anyone who tries to step into and block you from having a relationship with God through his son Jesus Christ does not do the Father's work but that of dark powers. Fortunately, we have not been left helpless or without protection. Let us each in our faith be empowered to put on the full regalia of that armor given to us so that we can stand firm against those who try to block you from God and from Jesus.

There's the buckle of truth that Jesus is the savior for all of us, LG-BTQ+ people included; the breastplate of righteousness that covers our hearts from the piercing swords of their hurtful words that seek to exclude us. Remember, our case and our cause for inclusion in the body of Christ are righteous!

We have feet fitted in the gospel of peace because nothing can move us from what God has given us; the shield that thwarts all the fiery arrows that are thrown our way, even from those who proclaim Jesus; the helmet of salvation, which thankfully is large enough that even my biggest curl of red hair can get tucked right up under, because we are the very people Jesus came to save, the outcasts.

Finally, my friends, pick up that sword of the Spirit, which is the word of God. Study it yourself. Do not rely on the words, interpretations, and screaming fits of other men and allow these to take the place of what God himself declares.

Of course, we are asked to turn the other cheek to people like the American evangelical who went off on me for being a gay drag queen Christian. But this does not mean God has left us defenseless weaklings who should cower in the corner. We have a powerful set of weaponry. One is not a passive bystander when one yields a sword and shield. One fights back accordingly when they need to, especially for the weak and the voiceless. This includes for our own community, which is under constant attack for just existing.

Jesus said, "I am the way and the truth and the life" (John 14:6) and "the truth shall make you free" (John 8:32 KJV).

If you are thinking about following Jesus but unsure if he has a place in his kingdom for you; if you are a Christian already but struggle with whether or not God is still on your side because of your sexuality or gender; if you came to this devotional book simply seeking to better understand your place in God's plan, I will close where I opened.

God is there for you. Embracing Christ as the savior is primary. Putting God first in your life is right at the tippy top. Loving your neighbor as yourself is secondary. Your sexuality and gender are way down there, if even on the list at all.

There is a place for us. Absolutely no man alive except for the one who has risen himself can take that seat that is ours at his table away.

Draw close to God, and embrace the love, peace, hope, joy, and freedom that is in Jesus Christ, which are not predicated on who you are attracted to, what genitalia you wield in your knickers, or which pronouns you ascribe to.

Stand firm in your faith, and God will stand firm with you.

PRAYER

Heavenly Father. Thank you for leaving me with powerful weaponry and armor with which I can withstand the attacks against my faith in you. I pray, dear Lord, that I draw closer to you, because the words and deeds of others, no matter who they are and what they say, cannot separate me from your love.

REFLECTION

1. How has this devotional book changed me or my outlook on God?

2. Where in my life am I prepared to stand more firm moving forward?

3. What are the next steps for me in my faith in Jesus?

Afterword

I hope you are now "juiced" up to go out and do your thing as an LGBTQ+ Christian or ally! Wherever you are at and whatever you identify as, may your first and last identity ultimately be anchored in Christ.

Heels off to you for going on this devotional journey with me. I leave you with a prayer:

May the God of Abraham, Isaac, and Jacob reveal himself to you as you walk closer to him each day. May you be blessed with love for your friends, family, allies, enemies, and yourself.

May you find true abundance and happiness that only comes from a deep and abiding relationship with the All-Knowing. Finally, may you recognize your value, exactly as you are, to the creator.

I pray these things in the name of the one who came for all of us, most definitely and especially including every member of the LGBTQ+ community, our Lord and Savior, Jesus Christ.

Amen.

JEZA'S JESUS JUICE COCKTAIL RECIPE

- Pour 1.5 shots of coconut rum, 1 ounce of coconut milk, 7 ounces of pineapple juice, and 2 ounces of orange juice into a blender filled with ice and blend.
- Add to a large glass.
- Add 2 ounces of cherry syrup. Give it a very light stir to swirl the cherry syrup.
- Add 1 additional shot of white rum as a floater
- Garnish with a cherry, pineapple slice, and a hail Mary, as girl, you're gonna need it! These are so delicious they sneak up on you!

*For the mocktail, add 2.5 ounces of coconut milk instead of rum.